S0-EDB-334

PEOPLE and OTHER MAMMALS

Books by George Laycock

THE ALIEN ANIMALS

ANIMAL MOVERS

THE DEER HUNTER'S BIBLE

THE DILIGENT DESTROYERS

THE PELICANS

THE SHOTGUNNER'S BIBLE

THE SIGN OF THE FLYING GOOSE

WILD REFUGE

STRANGE MONSTERS AND GREAT SEARCHES

PEOPLE AND OTHER MAMMALS

PEOPLE and OTHER MAMMALS

George Laycock

Doubleday & Company, Inc.

Garden City, New York

1975

Printed in the United States of America
First Edition

Library of Congress Cataloging in Publication Data

Laycock, George.
People and other mammals.

SUMMARY: Discusses the common characteristics of a variety of mammals and their relationship with man.
1. Mammals—Juvenile literature. [1. Mammals]
I. Title.
QL706.2.L39 599
ISBN 0-385-00179-7 Trade
0-385-00227-0 Prebound
Library of Congress Catalog Card Number 74-4874

ACKNOWLEDGMENTS

The author is grateful for help given him by numerous scientists during the preparation of this book, and to others as well who have shared with him their observations. In particular he wishes to express his appreciation to the editors and publishers of *Boys' Life, Field and Stream,* and *Farm Quarterly* for granting permission to include materials which originally appeared in somewhat different form in their publications.

CONTENTS

PEOPLE and OTHER MAMMALS

Gray squirrels are expert tree climbers. (George Laycock)

Chapter 1

THE MAMMAL WORLD

From the windows in my house I look down upon a woods and little creek, the home of wild creatures I have come to know. There are always the birds with their flashing colors and bubbling songs, orioles, vireos, mockingbirds, wrens, towhees, and others. Sometimes on winter nights I hear the throaty hooting songs of great horned owls that nest in an ancient broken sugar maple down by the creek.

But the woodland is also the home of mammals, and these are special favorites. Gray squirrels scamper through the trees making wild, impossible leaps from limb to limb. Beneath the leaves on the forest floor live the tiny mice and shrews. After dark the red fox trots along the creek on his evening hunting trips. I know the waddling raccoon has splashed through the shallow water because I have seen his tracks on the creekbank.

Perhaps one reason the mammals are favorites of so many people is because people are mammals too. We

The waddling raccoon eats a wide variety of food, both animal and vegetable. (George Laycock)

have much in common with the squirrels, raccoons, and the foxes. As mammals, we are members of the most advanced group of animals in the world.

How do mammals differ from the other creatures? It is not because mammals have backbones. So do the birds, reptiles, amphibians, and fishes.

There are two things that make mammals especially different. Only mammals have hair, although some have little if any. Because of hair, which can either retain heat or allow it to escape, mammals can survive in a wide variety of climates ranging from the tropics to the polar regions. All mammals, and only mammals, feed their young a special fluid from the mother's body, milk. These then are the characteristics that really set the mammals apart from all other animals; hair and milk.

The world's mammals are divided into three groups, monotremes, marsupials, and placentals. Most of the mammals, including man, belong to the last subclass, the placentals. This is the group whose young are born after becoming fully developed inside the mother's body. The marsupials are known for the pouches in which they carry their young. Among these are the kangaroos of Australia, and the opossum. Their young, after they are born, complete their development within these pouches. But the smallest group of all, and perhaps the most remarkable, are the monotremes. These mammals, like most reptiles, lay eggs from which their young develop. The best-known monotreme is the platypus.

Scientists believe that mammals evolved from reptiles

Foxes are alert and sensitive to the world around them. (Walter Lauffer, Ohio Division of Wildlife)

in the distant past when the earth was still ruled by dinosaurs and other reptiles. The climate was warm and there were vast swamps and marshes. But then, across thousands of years, the climate changed gradually and many living creatures had to change too. Those that could not adapt became extinct. The climate continued to change. The world grew colder. Mountains were lifted up.

Those earliest mammals developing to meet these changes were small creatures, perhaps rat-sized. The huge flesh-eating reptiles still lumbered over the earth while tiny primitive mammals hid for safety.

Where inland seas had stood, the land rose slowly. It became colder and drier. The world was no longer so well suited to the cold-blooded reptiles. In time, mammals would come to dominate the earth just as the huge reptiles had once done. The cooling drier climate brought broad fields of grasslands reaching away to the horizons, and mammals evolved in great variety. Teeth changed and great herds of grazing creatures evolved and fed on the grass.

Other mammals evolved in such a manner they could live only in the water, and needed water to support the weight of their bodies. Among these are the whales and the manatees. The seals and sea lions also live much of their lives in water, but can still come out on land part of the time. Meanwhile there are mammals living under the surface of the earth, on the earth, in the trees, and in the skies—moles, rabbits, squirrels, and bats, to name a few.

There are very big mammals and tiny mammals. The

Sea lions and seals live much of their lives in the water. (George Laycock)

shrew may weigh a fraction of an ounce. The giant blue whale may weigh 130 tons and grow far bigger than any dinosaur ever did. There are mammals to eat almost all kinds of plants as well as other animals.

How many kinds of mammals inhabit the world? Scientists counting all the known species place the figure at nearly 4,300.

The wide world of mammals is filled with surprises and discoveries for all who would explore their remarkable life stories.

Chapter 2

THE LITTLE ONES

When you are resting on a log in the woods, and there is a rustling of the leaves at your feet, you may be about to meet one of the smallest mammals in the world. The meeting, however, will probably be brief. A tiny pointed snout pushes quickly up through the dead leaves, twitches nervously, then vanishes just as suddenly as it appeared. The chances are you have just seen a shrew, which, in spite of its featherweight standing, is among the world's most successful predators.

For many years scientists knew little about the shrews. These tiny secretive mammals are content to stay out of sight. They dwell in the underworld where their lives are spent dashing about through a maze of dark subways. Gradually, however, naturalists pieced together their amazing life story.

These cousins of the moles are found throughout the world, except for Australia and the southern half of South America. There are about fifty species of them, and all of them have similar, pointed snouts, tiny, pinhead-sized eyes, and ears so small and hidden beneath their fur that they seem not to be there at all. Shrews dash about on short legs and have short tails. Their fur is so soft and velvety that it brushes both ways, forward if the animal is backing up in its burrow, and backward when the shrew runs forward.

Most shrews are smaller than mice. The short-tailed shrew is about the size of a house mouse, and other shrews are considerably smaller yet. For example, the least shrew is so small that seven of them weigh an ounce. But the pigmy shrew holds the real honors. Each of these unbelievable midgets, when fully grown, is about equal to the weight of a dime.

They may be small but the shrews rank with the most fearless fighters in the animal world. Their tiny jaws are equipped with sharp-edged teeth. Snapping at their victims with lightning speed, they slice off portions, sometimes even before the victim is dead. Shrews are driven by a hunger that will not stop. Their stomachs must be stoked with fuel hour after hour as long as the shrew is alive. A shrew can starve to death within a day. It must have at least the equivalent of its own weight in meat each day, and sometimes it may eat several times its weight in a single day.

This forces the tiny shrew to be a mighty hunter. Mostly its foods are insects, but it also eats millepedes, worms, grubs, and even snails which it removes from the shells by cutting a small hole in the side. If these foods are in short supply, and the shrew corners a mouse in its tunnel, the shrew may attack it in spite of the fact that it is only half the size of the mouse.

A least shrew eating a cricket. (Karl H. Maslowski)

If the mouse can escape and dash away, it would be well advised to do so. The darting form of the tiny shrew hesitates. The pointed snout is lifted and the whiskers twitch. The shrew picks up the scent and charges in a bold frontal attack.

Years ago naturalists learned that the shrew has more than sharp teeth and lightning swiftness to help it make a kill. Ordinarily a man can handle shrews without being injured because the shrew has a difficult time getting a grip on a man's skin. But on one occasion a short-tailed shrew nipped the hand of a naturalist. At first the bite seemed scarcely anything at all. The naturalist ignored the little cut—but not for long. Soon he noticed a burning sensation around the bite. Then his hand began to swell. Shooting pains reached up his arm. The soreness in his arm lasted a full week.

But this opened up a new possibility. Dr. Oliver Pearson began investigating the strange power of the shrew. He extracted fluids from the salivary glands of the little animals. Then he injected some of these fluids into the body of an unfortunate laboratory mouse. Almost at once the mouse began having tremors. Then paralysis spread through its body. The mouse was soon dead. Now it was known that the short-tailed shrew, and perhaps other species too, use poison on their victims. The poison carried by the short-tailed shrew seems similar to that of the cobra, and the average shrew carries enough of this venom to kill two hundred mice.

At first, when attacked by a shrew, the mouse may fight back. The match seems to favor the mouse. But the shrew moves with a speed that is marvelous to behold. The embattled mouse begins to look sluggish and tired. When the shrew gets a nip into the neck or shoulder of the mouse, the battle is as good as finished.

Even shrews may not be safe from other shrews, especially when supplies of food run low. Dr. C. Hart Merriam once placed three common shrews together as a test. One of the shrews was promptly killed and consumed. Now there were two, each of them eying its neighbor hungrily. When hunger again rose in the little shrews, the battle was on. At the end of the drama three shrews had become one—and all within a brief eight hours.

Most shrews live in the moist forests, although some live in grasslands or in the tundra of the North Country, and others in the deserts. There is even a shrew that is a water lover, and it is called a "water shrew." It is seldom found more than a few yards from streams or ponds. These are the only mammals capable of running on water. With air trapped in their fur and pockets of air forming bubbles under their feet, they can scamper across a brook.

They also swim beneath the surface, darting here and there in search of aquatic foods. Sometimes the water shrew finds trout eggs for its lunch, or it may catch and consume a meal of tiny baby trout. If all this sounds like a fun-filled world for a little fur-covered water lover, remember that the water shrew has enemies too. It may no sooner catch a little trout than a big trout catches it, which seems fair enough.

Meanwhile the shrews out there in the woods and fields also face enemies. Their names are on the long list of small creatures that go to feed the birds of prey, snakes, foxes, and other flesh eaters.

During the summer a female shrew may have two or three litters of young and give birth to half a dozen bumblebee-sized infants each time. Her young are born about three weeks after the mating, and within a few days the mother mates again. The young, born blind, naked, and helpless, are as big as their parents within a month.

Not surprisingly, shrews grow old quickly. They lead a fast life, hour on hour, day after day. They never learn how to relax. By the time they are fourteen months old they are likely to die—of old age. But a shrew should have no regrets. It has lived life to the fullest, the only way a shrew knows to live.

Chapter 3

UNDERGROUND MAMMALS

Down at the grassroots the common mole pushes his way through his little dark world, unaware of the fact that people up there do not like him much.

They do not like what he does to their front yards, their tulip beds, and their carrot patches. And they hate him for what he does to golf courses. What the mole does is push the turf up into little ridges that send golf balls on detours. Instead of dropping into a hole in the ground, the ball may veer off in some completely new direction, providing the golfers an excellent excuse for a poor shot.

As for the mole, he does not need an excuse. He is only going about his hidden life precisely as moles did long before golf courses were invented. His world is well ordered, his hazards are few. As long as bugs and grubs and worms hold out, the mole is likely to lead a good life.

Moles are well designed for their cave dweller's life. Their velvety fur is so soft that it slides along the walls of tunnels smoothly. A mole hears fairly well, but to look at one you might not suspect this. Its ears are hidden inside its pointed little head and are equipped with cut-off valves that keep the dirt out of them.

Some moles are almost blind. They can barely tell light from dark. But blindness is no tragedy to a mole; where he lives it is dark all the time anyhow and he may never leave home. In his naked nose and tail he has nerve endings, sending messages to his brain if he bumps into obstructions. Two kinds of moles, the star-nose and shrew mole, often come out of their tunnels to search for food.

Moles are well equipped for their underground work. They have broad, strong shoulders to help them loosen and move earth. Their front feet are digging tools. Claws dig the soil loose, and the broad, shovel-like feet push it like bulldozers. With this earth-moving equipment a mole can dig tunnels at the rate of twelve to fifteen feet an hour, even if he stops now and then to rest or to eat an earthworm.

Homes of the common moles usually have an upstairs and a downstairs. Those tunnels just beneath the grass in the front yard are where moles come to eat. But they rest and raise their young in tunnels six to twenty-four inches beneath the surface.

They usually avoid sandy soils for at least two reasons. In the first place there are not as many worms and bugs there to eat as they find in fertile soils, rich in humus. The other reason is because sand caves in easily and they would have to spend too much time repairing the roofs of their tunnels.

The mole's velvety fur allows it to move easily through its burrows.
(George Laycock)

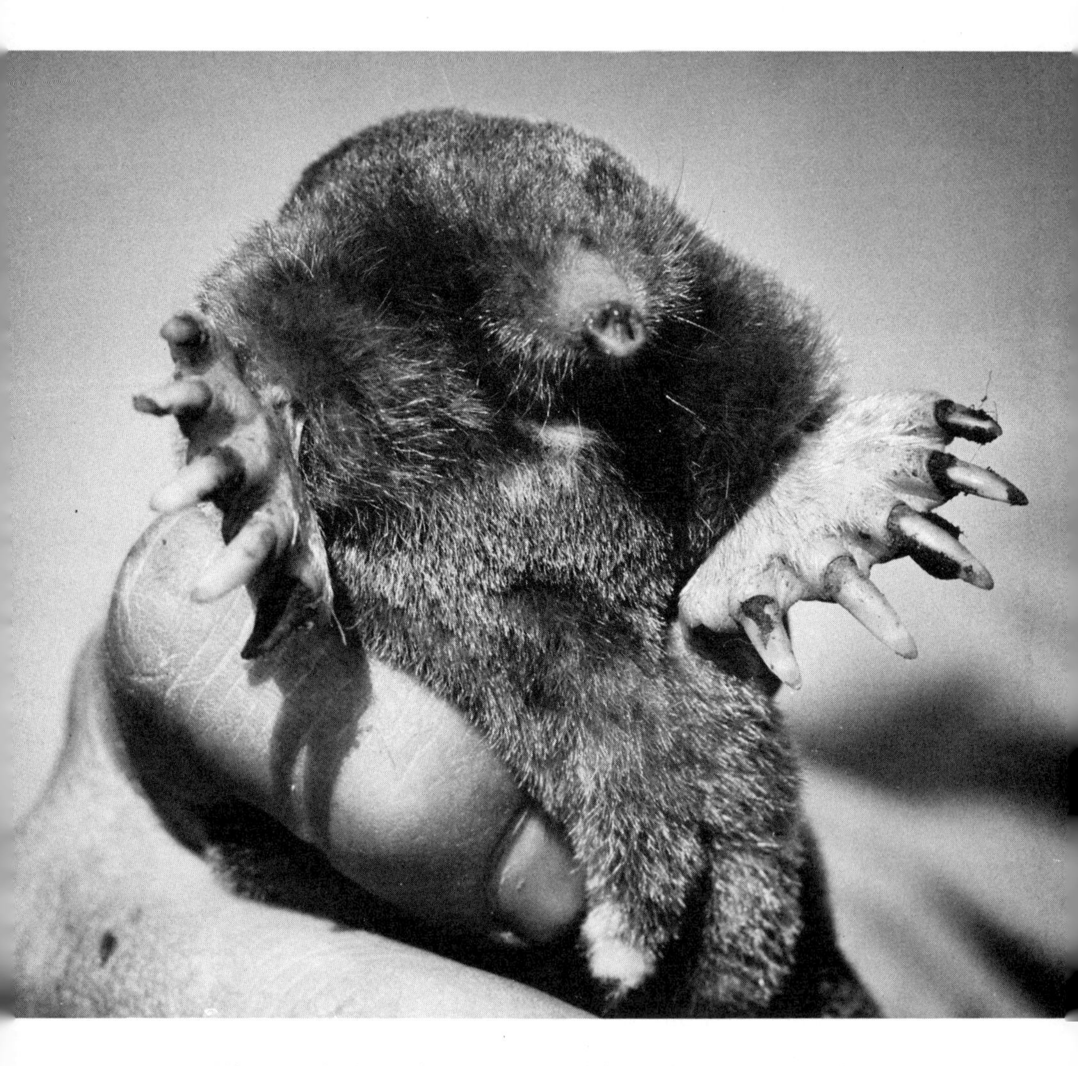

The mole's front feet are powerful digging tools. (Karl H. Maslowski)

Moles live alone and apparently prefer it that way. Male and female alike live as hermits except for a brief period in early spring during the breeding season. The female will have only one litter of three or four young each year. Field mice, by contrast, have young as fast as they can produce them, then their young grow up quickly and produce young of their own, all in an endless effort to stay ahead of the predators and elements. But a mouse leads a life far different from that of a mole. Mice are up there chasing around in the grass. And every time a mouse moves, there may be a screech owl, fox, or weasel to see it. Down among the moles, the hazards are fewer, and a mole may live for as long as three years.

His life, however, is not entirely free of danger. Hawks, snakes, foxes, and skunks catch moles if they can. Moles drown when lawns and fields are flooded. Drought may send the earthworms so deep that hungry moles can find no underground food and must go outdoors to hunt insects. There the predators can catch them.

But the mole's worst enemy is man. Who else would think to shoot poison gas into the mole's tunnel? What other creature would set ingenious traps over his runways, or watch the grass until it moves, then run with a long-handled shovel and quickly scoop the mole out and kill it?

But moles can cause a lot of trouble. They cut through tulip bulbs and deform carrots. Sometimes they push up against young corn plants and lift them until the roots come loose and the plants die.

If the mole's roof caves in, it is quickly repaired. People who know this sometimes press the roof of a mole tunnel down with a foot. Then if the ridge is raised again, this is a promising place to set a mole trap.

The trap most commonly used has a metal pan to rest against the top of the soil where it has been tramped down. The mole crawling along the dark tunnel discovers the caved-in roof and goes to work at once. It lifts the earth back into place. This lifts the pan on the trap, releasing the trigger. Long spikes plunge into the soil and the mole.

In America the littlest mole of all is the shrew mole, only four and a half inches long. This tiny cave dweller lives in the coastal country of the Pacific Northwest. Unlike its eastern cousins, it piles earth up outside its tunnels. This is not always a good plan because it serves as a tip-off to the people who kill moles.

Chapter 4

MAMMALS THAT FLY

Of all the mammals in the world, the bats are the only ones capable of flight. The flying squirrel is a pretty good glider, but it doesn't dare try what the bats do. Those bats you see maneuvering over the neighborhood in the soft evening light come from a clan that has known the freedom of true flight for millions of years. They are at ease on the wing, flitting through the darkness, avoiding trees, fences, television antennas, and volley ball nets with remarkable skill. A bat can half-fold one wing or both, fly forward, backward, or hover, and this is only the beginning of its long list of accomplishments.

Around the world there are about two thousand species of bats. They range in size from the tiny bamboo bat of Southeast Asia weighing perhaps an eighth of an ounce, to the giant flying foxes of Java with a wing-spread of four feet. We usually think of bats as being insect eaters, and many of them are. But there are also bats that catch fish for a living, some that live on fruit, and others that search out flowers and eat the nectar.

Meanwhile, the famous vampire bats of Central and South America live on a liquid diet; fresh blood which they obtain by slicing into the skin of poultry, sheep, goats, cattle, horses, and people.

As for the insect-eating bats, these are the species most welcome around our homes and farms. Each night they flutter out of the dark places and pass back and forth over the landscape capturing enough mosquitoes, moths, and other insects to equal a third or more of their body weight.

How do bats manage to fly so expertly no matter how dark the night? One might think the secret is in their eyes. Scientists speculated about this for many years. Then one investigator worked out tests which he hoped would tell him the answers.

First he caught some bats and brought them into his laboratory. Then he suspended many wires from the ceiling. He covered the eyes of a bat so it could not see, then turned it loose in the room filled with hanging wires. The unseeing bat performed perfectly, flying skillfully around the room as it tilted, stopped, turned, and changed courses in a remarkable display of acrobatics.

Next the scientist plugged up the bat's ears. Suddenly the bat began colliding with a large percentage of the wires. Finally the scientist also sealed the bat's ears and mouth shut. Now the little flying mammal was in real trouble, even when its eyes were left uncovered.

Obviously the bat was hearing something as it flew.

The scientist had learned for the first time that the sounds the bat heard were also made by it. The bat was sending out sound waves, then listening to the echoes. These sounds, however, were not at a frequency the human ear could detect.

Eventually bats were tested in a laboratory where a sensitive microphone picked up the sounds they made. The microphone was attached to an oscilloscope, an electronic device that transforms the energy of the ultrasonic sound waves into lines flashed on a screen. The mystery was solved. The bat was sending high-pitched sound waves against every object in front of it, and the echoes were bouncing back telling it the location of obstructions in its path. This principle, new to man, has been used by bats for millions of years.

Sometimes you may have the opportunity to look closely at one of our common bats. Consider its remarkable wing. The bones of the arm are long and slender and the fingers have lengthened out of all proportion. Stretching between the fingers, and between the arm and the body, is a membrane of naked skin, the wing covering. The whole structure is beautifully strong and flexible, and large enough to carry the bat's small body in silent and graceful motion for hours at a time.

Then look at the end of the bat's feet where it carries another piece of special equipment. Each foot has a clawlike hook. This works out very well because bats need it for hanging themselves upside down in a cave, tree, or attic when they want to rest or hibernate.

A bat burns great amounts of energy in flight as it

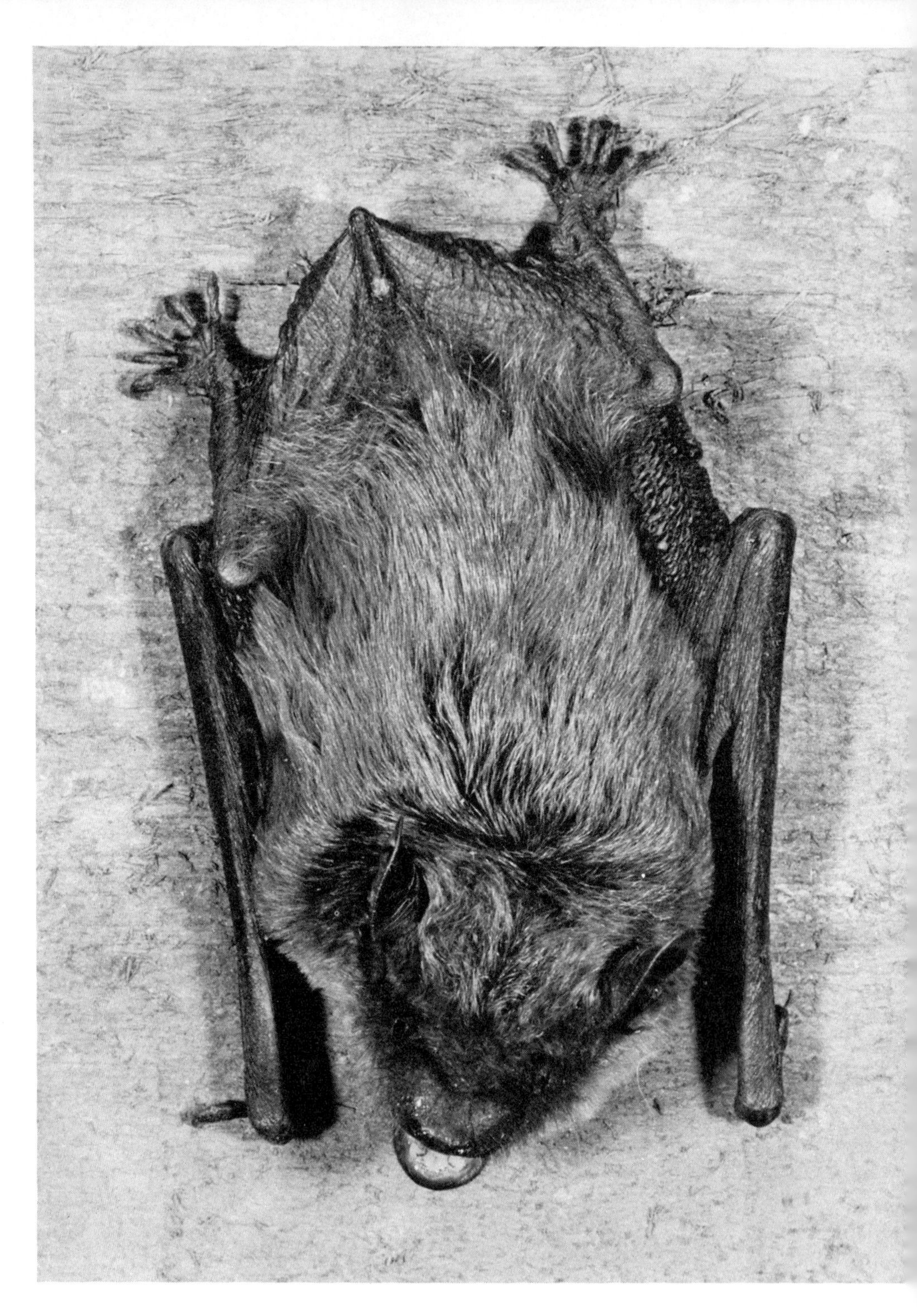

The big brown bat hangs upside down to sleep. (Karl H. Maslowski)

gathers food. Its heart beats rapidly, its rate of breathing increases, and its metabolism is high. But the feeding spree may last only an hour or two. Then it's back to the cave, tree, or church steeple, to rest. There the well-fed, furry, little beast hooks himself to the ceiling again and the life processes start to slow down. Its heart soon quiets to only a few beats a minute. Its rate of breathing slows. In winter, when it hibernates, the bat may hang there, almost motionless week after week.

Caves are the normal places for hibernating bats to spend their winters. Clusters of them blacken the ceiling with little furry bodies. They may have occupied temporary summer quarters in an old building, then gathered from a hundred miles around for their winter together in the cave.

Some bats, instead of hibernating, migrate south as winter comes on, and, in this manner, live the year around where the weather is warm, and the insects abundant.

In the wild a bat may live for several years. A friend of mine, a professor who is an authority on bats, once told me, "If people lived the way bats do, you and I might live to be a thousand years old." A long time to hang by one's toes.

In spring, when the female bat gives birth to one or two tiny, helpless young, these babies hang onto her teats by their little teeth. For the first few days they may even ride along in this fashion, also gripping her fur with their feet, as she flies out of the cave to cruise the skies for food. Soon, however, they are too heavy and she has to leave them at home, hanging up bat fashion, while she goes hunting.

For some reason people have strange ideas about bats. If, for example, you hear that bats will fly into a person's long hair, don't believe it. Why in the world would a bat do that? Or you may be told that bats are covered with lice, mites, and other parasites that will hop off onto people. Many bats do carry these little free-loaders. But these parasites have been getting along on bats for millions of years, and as unbelievable as it may seem to us, they seem to prefer bats.

If you hear that some bats carry rabies, however, you are hearing the truth. It is possible for a rabid bat to bite a person and infect him with this deadly virus.

What if bats begin living where you do not want them, for example, the attic of your home? Do not kill them. Wait instead until evening. Watch where they come out. Then, while they are gone, cover the holes with screen. This way the bats are still alive, flying around at night, eating mosquitoes.

Chapter 5

RABBITS EVERYWHERE

The rabbit has few claims to fame. He is not a spectacular fighter, nor does he make long migrations. He does not bark like a fox, build dams like a beaver, burrow like a groundhog, or even climb trees like a squirrel.

And as for appearance, his fur coat is commonplace when compared with mink or even muskrat. His color is monotonously dull, and his size is modest. The rabbit's ears are out of proportion to the rest of him. And for a tail he has a ridiculous little white powderpuff which serves no useful purpose known to man except to give the rabbit its name—cottontail.

But the rabbit, for all his bland character and mild way of living, is nearly always welcome around home and farm. He is welcomed by people who like to hunt, hounds who like to hunt, foxes who like to hunt, and owls, hawks, coyotes, bobcats, and a lengthy list of other creatures who like to hunt.

For the cottontail, life may begin with a strange

The cottontail provides food for numerous predators. (R. Radford, United States Soil Conservation Service)

courtship dance in the moonlight. Once the rabbits have mated, the female soon turns viciously on the male and drives him from the territory. She asks no help with the home duties and receives none.

The rabbit nursery is a bowl-shaped hollow, excavated in the meadow or lawn. It may have begun with some slight depression the female found already there, or she may prepare it from the beginning. And once the bowl is completed, she pulls soft fur from her belly to line the nest. Then she pulls a blanket of grass and fur across the top and hides her preparations until the young arrive.

Unfortunately, she may have made the nest several days before it is needed. This is all right in dry weather. But if the nest should get soaked the rabbit may return and give birth to her young in the damp bed. Early spring rains cause large numbers of little rabbits to die by drowning and exposure.

The young are born twenty-eight days after the parents have mated. Generally there are four or five of them in the litter. They weigh about one ounce each. Most females produce three or four litters during spring and summer. During daylight hours she stays away from her nest, perhaps resting nearby but not daring to go near her young, because a predator might see her and find her helpless family. After dark the mother returns to feed her young ones.

When the little rabbits are about two weeks old, they are furry little copies of their parents. Now they are ready to venture from the family nest. Shortly they are sampling green foods and adding salads to their milk diet.

Their new world is filled with wonders. Gradually, they move farther and farther from the nest. As they grow up they spread out into nearby fields where there may be enough food and cover and not too many rabbits. In this manner the vacant niches are refilled and rabbits keep the earth populated with rabbits.

But if life for a rabbit is filled with wonders, it is also filled with dangers. Biologists believe that fully a third of the young rabbits do not live long enough to leave the nest. Weather, predators, parasites, and man, along with his machines, cats, and dogs all take their toll of the young rabbits.

Winter can be especially hard on rabbits. A slight crust of snow will support the rabbit's weight, but a fluffy snow can bog him down and make him easy for predators to catch. Snow may also seal away the winter food where the rabbits cannot reach it, and the rabbits starve.

Rabbits are not distance runners, but on the short dash they can stay ahead of the beagle hounds. Rout a cottontail from his form where he rests during the day, and he dashes off in a frenzy, makes frantic right-angle turns, scoots through the weed patch, visible one moment, out of sight the next. Then he slips beneath a brush pile or scurries down an abandoned burrow left by some other animal. The chase is over, at least for the moment.

Cottontails are reluctant to leave their home territories. Instead of getting far away when chased, they

Severe winter weather can be especially hard on rabbits. (Karl H. Maslowski)

travel in circular paths. Rabbit hunters know this well. So while their short-legged beagle hounds gaily trail the cottontail, the hunter stands and waits. Sooner or later the dog brings the rabbit back past him again.

Perhaps the most celebrated rabbits in history belonged to Thomas Austin, who moved to Australia where there were no rabbits. He decided in 1859 that what his Australian ranch needed were some European rabbits to provide sport for him and his beagles. He sent back to England for twenty pairs, and his rabbits arrived on the ship *Lightning* in time to be set free in Australia on Christmas Day.

Australians soon wished they had never received these rabbits as a Christmas gift. Only ten years after the rabbits' arrival, Austin estimated that he had killed twenty thousand and another ten thousand still were hopping around the neighborhood.

Then his rabbits began crossing the borders of his ranch and spreading over the Australian countryside. They destroyed grasslands while sheep went hungry, and the sheep industry began to fail. The rabbits also caused great soil erosion.

These rabbits are a different species from the American cottontails. In their native lands rabbits as well as other native animals are kept in check by predators and diseases that have evolved with them. In Australia, however, the European rabbits were suddenly free of the natural enemies which help nature maintain her balances. This mistake cost Australians millions of dollars.

Sometimes our native cottontails move into our gardens and help themselves to the lettuce and cabbage.

A cottontail eating multiflora rose hips. (Karl H. Maslowski)

They know a good thing when they find it. This raiding of the garden may make enemies for them among people. But perhaps the loss of an occasional plant is not too high a price to pay for having the furry, long-eared rabbits for neighbors.

Chapter 6

THE PLAYFUL DOLPHIN

If you have traveled much at sea you probably know the dolphins or porpoises, and once you have seen these graceful, dashing mammals of the open oceans you do not easily forget them. One moment there may be only the calm, unbroken surface of the water. Then a dark torpedo-shaped creature, perhaps ten feet long, rises from the water, curves gracefully, and dips back into its element with scarcely a splash. There may be a group of them, little cousins of the great whales, traveling together, leaping and spinning in their marine ballet. Down through the ages people have never grown tired of watching them.

For example, I was standing one sunny afternoon on the bow of a large fishing boat. We were plowing through the smooth Caribbean Sea when a pair of porpoises appeared to starboard and knifed from the water. Next, they rushed in on the boat as if they fully intended to ram it. They turned quickly and streaked alongside like dark miniature submarines.

Then they took positions directly in front of the boat and kept their speed exactly equal to ours. From time to time, they turned aside, rushed around the boat, then returned to take up their positions of leadership.

They played this game for perhaps a quarter of an hour. Then they turned away and vanished to do whatever it is porpoises do when there are no boats for them to play around.

These mammals of the oceans, like many other wild creatures, are being threatened by man's activities. No one knows how many porpoises there are in the world, but we do know that they are being killed so rapidly that they may be in danger of extinction. Their biggest losses come from commercial tuna fishermen. Tuna fishermen do not want to harm the porpoises but they do not always know how they can help them.

Most of the porpoises that die because of tuna fishing belong to only two species of the many kinds of porpoises known. And these losses are mostly in the Pacific, in the eastern tropical yellowfin tuna fishery.

This trouble for porpoises exists because tuna and porpoises travel together. Once the fisherman find the porpoises, they have also found the tuna. Why? Perhaps because both porpoises and the yellowfin tuna feed on the same small species of fish. Tuna fishermen know to set out their half-mile long nets quickly when they see porpoises. Then powerful winches begin to tighten the net around the school of tuna.

Caught in this trap also, the highly sensitive porpoises panic as they crowd away from the tightening net. They seem not to realize that they could easily race up to it and leap over the top to freedom, a simple matter for these seagoing acrobats.

But the tightening net is a death trap growing steadily closer to them. The porpoises are mammals and must have air to breathe. Finally they are held beneath the surface hopelessly entangled in the nylon net. There they drown. Perhaps a quarter of a million porpoises drown in this way every year. Those species facing the most serious trouble in the tuna nets are spinner and spotted porpoises.

To this add several thousand more porpoises taken for food. There was a time when the porpoise, fat and oily, was popular human food in many places. In the days of Henry VIII this was a dish fit for a king. Today the kill for food continues in Japan. They are taken there in autumn when herds of porpoises are migrating southward.

Once the traveling porpoises are discovered, fishermen in boats rush out to herd them into protected coves. How do you herd a porpoise? This is accomplished with underwater sound made by pounding on pipes held in the water. The porpoises panic. Once the herd, which may number several hundred animals, is inside the cove, a strong net is stretched behind them to cut off their escape route. Now the porpoises can be lifted out of the water by a winch and killed. This, according to the Japanese government, accounts for eleven thousand to sixteen thousand porpoises a year.

There are about forty species of porpoises. Some people call certain species of them dolphins. They belong to the whale family. Perhaps best known of them all is the Atlantic bottlenose dolphin. These are the clowns often seen in marine shows, tossing balls to people, leaping through blazing hoops, and towing little dogs on surf boards.

The common porpoise will weigh about 120 pounds. Its jaws are lined with rows of sharp teeth. Like all the toothed whales, porpoises have a single blowhole in the top of their heads. Their size and colors vary among the species. The common porpoise sometimes seen along the coast in the New England states may live as long as thirty years.

The breeding season comes in summer, and the female gives birth to a single young porpoise about eleven months later. This newborn young one already has a good start in life and is about half as long as its mother. Most mammals come into the world head first, but not the porpoise. Instead it comes tail first from its mother's body. This helps guard it against drowning at the time of birth. Now another porpoise arrives to help the new mother raise her baby. Together the two older porpoises, the mother and the baby sitter, which stays on the job for several weeks, may move the newborn youngster to the surface for its first breath of air. The mother, while drifting on her side in the open sea, feeds her young one on milk, and it grows rapidly.

Porpoises fascinate people. Scientists study them in all manner of experiments. U. S. Navy scientists want to know more about their remarkable ability to communicate under water.

Meanwhile we hope to discover ways to save the porpoises from death in the tuna nets. There may be a

The white whales, or belugas, are Arctic mammals that live in the ocean. (George Laycock)

clue in an experiment tried in Alaska. Thousands of salmon crowd into rivers there to spawn, and then the white whales, or belugas, cousins of the better-known dolphins, may arrive in the rivers and feast on the salmon. Experimenters broadcast the recorded sounds of the deadly killer whales through the water, and this made the belugas turn and flee for the safety of the open seas.

But the most determined efforts to protect the porpoises from the fishing nets are centered around the activities of government researchers in the National Marine Fisheries Service. Recently these scientists, employed by the U. S. Department of Commerce, have been going to sea with the tuna fishermen. Aboard a tuna fishing boat, the *Patricia Lee,* they have studied all the latest methods of protecting the porpoises from the encircling nets. Nets that sink faster, small power boats to keep the nets open, and other ideas have all been put to use. Captains of tuna ships have attended classes to learn better ways to save the porpoises. These steps have helped cut down the numbers of porpoises killed in the nets and have brought new laws to help the porpoises.

But these remarkable creatures of the sea are still in danger and biologists working to save them know their work is not yet complete.

Chapter 7

GIANTS OF THE SEA

As the creature rose to the surface, a fountain of air and water spouted from the top of its head, spraying twenty feet into the air. Then the old whale noticed the strange, clattering helicopter in the sky overhead. Alarmed, it slid down again into the depths of the ocean to hide in the gray shadows of its salt-water world. Unfortunately it had surfaced at the wrong time in the wrong place.

Above, the helicopter pilot radioed back to the factory ship. A few miles away a small, fast catch boat immediately roared into action. The catch boat, guided by the helicopter, closed in on the whale, and the giant mammal was suddenly in greater trouble than ever before in its life.

Whales, like all mammals, must breathe air, and they have no choice but to come to the surface. Slowly the giant whale's body used up its supply of oxygen. The men in the boat and helicopter waited.

When it could stand the pressure in its lungs no

longer, the whale surfaced. A rising fountain again sprayed from the top of its head and as it did, the gunner on the bow of the catch boat shot a harpoon. The whale was hit just behind the head. In the next instant the grenade in the tip of the harpoon exploded. As the struggling whale died, the catch boat took the creature in tow.

Next the body of the whale was alongside the larger ship. And thirty minutes later what had been one of the biggest animals in the world was processed and stored away.

Today the largest of all whales, the blue whale, is so rare the species is threatened with extinction. Nobody knows how many blue whales still swim the ocean waters, but scientists everywhere agree that there can be no more than three thousand. Their numbers may be much smaller, perhaps there are no more than five hundred. Some marine mammalogists belive this may be too small a number for the blue whales ever to rebuild their populations. They have been protected against whaling since 1965.

How big are these remarkable animals? The blue whale is the largest creature ever to live on earth, far bigger than the greatest of dinosaurs. Blue whales have reached lengths of 100 feet and weights estimated at 150 tons. Such a creature would weigh as much as 2,000 people, have a one-ton liver, and a heart which, by itself, might weigh 1,200 pounds.

When newborn the baby blue whale may already be twenty-three feet long. As if a three-ton baby is still too small, the mother begins at once pumping into her infant more than one hundred gallons daily of rich, nourishing milk. She does her job well. The baby grows so fast that by his first birthday he is sixty feet long from tip to tip. By the time the youthful monster is two and a half years old, he is already mature.

Through the ages the whales of the oceans have developed into two kinds, those with teeth and those without. Instead of teeth, such species as the blue whale, the humpback and the right whales have curtains of fibers in their mouths hanging from their upper jaw bones. These screens of baleen are their sieves, and the whales need them because they eat such small foods.

At certain seasons, the oceans come alive with microscopic plants. These are consumed by masses of small shrimplike creatures. Then as the shrimp or krill grow, they cover the surface of the ocean, and the giant baleen whales come to fatten on them.

Now the blue whale swims through the masses of krill, and its giant trap-door jaws open and close. Using a tongue that may weigh four tons, it pushes excess water out through the sides of its cavelike mouth. But the food it has scooped from the ocean can't escape those baleen strainers. Next, the giant tongue forces the food down the whale's throat.

Meanwhile, the whales equipped with teeth are hunting big game. They dine on fish, seals, and even other whales. There is nothing dainty about their eating habits. Perhaps the most feared of the world's toothed whales, at least among the ancient whalers, was the sperm whale. These giants were unpredictable when whaling boats pursued them. They sometimes rammed the small boats pursuing them and were known to catch these boats in their great jaws and bite them in two, occupants and all.

There was a time when millions of whales of many species swam through the oceans of the world. Early hunters in their flimsy canoes were not much of a threat to them. But boats became bigger and faster. Man stepped up his attacks on the whales.

Then in 1868, a Norwegian inventor had a remarkable idea. He created a harpoon that carried an explosive bomb in its head. It was patented on Christmas Eve 1870, a grim Christmas gift for the world's whales.

Then the whaling industry built ships that were equipped to stay longer and longer at sea. Eventually there were factory ships with crews living aboard permanently, and with them were catch boats, electronic scanners, and finally helicopters for spotting, and whales could no longer hide in the oceans of the world. The hunting flourished until today only three species, the rorqual, sperm, and finback are left in numbers large enough to attract the whalers.

What do you do with a whale? A large percentage of the body is blubber and this is oil used for making lipsticks, shoe polish, margarine, and other products. The whale's bones are ground up for fertilizer. The meat goes for making cat food.

Before 1970, 20 per cent of the world's whale products came to the United States, but then Secretary of the Interior Walter J. Hickel moved to protect the whales of the world. He placed eight species of them, the right whale, finback, bowhead, blue, gray, humpback, sie, and sperm whales, all on the list of rare and endangered species. No longer was it legal to bring the products of these huge mammals into the United States.

But it is important for other nations to take similar action. Most of the whales killed today are taken by the boats of two countries, the Soviet Union and Japan. Authorities think that within ten years whaling may be finished completely because ships will no longer find enough whales to pay their owners to keep them on the seas.

We will then turn elsewhere and find substitutes for oil to use in lipstick, bones to use in fertilizer, and meat to feed our pet cats. But no matter how hard we search, we won't find substitutes for the living whales.

Chapter 8

BEARS AND PEOPLE

Somewhere far up a wooded mountainside in the Great Smokies an old black bear awakens in early spring, lean and grumpy. He yawns, stretches, sleeps some more, then awakens again. The hunger begins to grow inside him. Finally he moves out from his winter home where he slept in a den beneath the roots of a giant tree, and he begins walking slowly down the mountainside in the night.

He has reawakened for the summer, and chances are good that part of his food will come from picnic tables in the National Park. Park bears have learned that people carry food. The bears cannot be blamed for wanting a free meal, or at least a couple of cookies. But this close association of park bears and people sometimes causes more trouble for both bears and people than either of them want.

One visitor to the Great Smoky Mountains, who decided to take a nap in the bed of his pick-up truck,

A black bear awakens in early spring. (George Laycock)

had his pleasant dreams disturbed by a large black bear biting his foot.

When something like this happens, the park rangers have to stop whatever else they are doing and go after the bear. If it is a first offender, they may capture the animal and haul it several miles away, hoping it will not return to the scene of its crime. If it does come back, the offending bear may have to be killed.

Such bear problems have plagued the National Park Service for many years, especially in Yellowstone, Yosemite, and the Great Smoky Mountains. Bears are among the favorite wild creatures in these parks. Lines of cars come to a screeching halt in the middle of the highway whenever the drivers see a bear. Soon dozens of cameras are making hundreds of pictures. Finally, a ranger drives up and gets the traffic moving again.

Wild bears in the parks do not come to the camps and highways because they like people. Instead they like the food that people carry. One large bear in the Great Smokies smashed the windshield out of a locked car, found the picnic basket, and was seated on the hood having lunch when the owners returned from their hike. This, however, is a rare case, and it is still a good idea to lock food inside the car when camped in bear country.

Another pesky bear often recalled in the Great Smokies was a young animal whose specialty was climbing trees and edging out onto limbs above picnic tables. At the right moment it would, so the story goes, jump onto the middle of the table and all the people would scamper from the table and rush for their cars. Behind

People often take pictures of black bears from their cars. (George Laycock)

them, the contented bear helped himself to sandwiches and pie.

Under strictly natural conditions few people would ever see a bear. The black bear, in the wild, is shy and elusive, a creature of the back woods. It stays out of sight of people when possible, a good idea if it wants to keep that shaggy black fur coat.

When early settlers arrived on this continent, the black bear was found throughout most of the land. Bear meat became human food, and bear fur was also put to use. In addition, bears were killed to protect livestock. Often bears have been killed for little reason at all except that they wandered into a town or crossed the road in public view. Most black bears today are either in the parks where they are protected, or in the deep wilderness.

Mating season for the black bear usually comes about June. The young, often twins or triplets, are born seven months later while the female is denned up for the winter and sluggish with sleep. Her newborn cubs, weighing only half a pound, blind and helpless, cuddle into her long warm fur. The female ordinarily has new cubs every second year, and she may live twenty-five years if she stays out of trouble.

Like man, the black bear eats a wide variety of food including fish, fruits, vegetables, insects, birds, eggs, and small mammals depending on what can be found. When park bears emerge from their long winter's sleep which is not true hibernation, they may come to the roadsides to greet the tourists. There they attempt to open garbage cans and wander along the road waiting for someone to stop and give them a handout.

This is where the trouble starts. The more a bear is fed along the roadside, the more difficult it is for the animal to break the habit and go back to the old way of life, gathering its own provisions.

Meanwhile the park rangers realize that people and bears make an uneasy mixture and try to keep the two species separated. Feeding the park bears is illegal. There are signs warning visitors not to do it. But many people still break this rule and take a chance of being bitten or clawed. Bears are often impatient. If the food does not come fast enough, the bear may reach out, and with a lightning swift movement, gather in cookie, hand, and all. The Park Service has developed new bear-proof garbage cans to discourage the animals from their roadside picnics.

Most dangerous and unpredictable of the bears are the massive grizzlies. But these magnificent creatures are now so rare they are listed as endangered through most of their range south of Alaska. They are found in the back country both in Glacier and Yellowstone national parks. Rangers in these parks have the latest information on bears and hikers headed into the wilderness should first check with the rangers.

The best plan is not to get close to any bear, and especially not to take the animal by surprise. In grizzly country it is good practice to make noise as you hike along. Sing and whistle. The chances are the bears will slip off into the brush and stay hidden. And re-

Mating season for the black bear usually comes about June. (U. S. Forest Service)

member that, although black bears climb trees, the adult grizzly bears will not come up there after you.

Good campers try to outwit the bears in advance by keeping a clean camp. Bits of food, especially those that send tempting odors, attract bears. Keep garbage cleaned up and either sealed or burned. Food should be in airtight containers and hung out of the bears' reach. A deodorizer is a good camp item in bear country.

Most of all, follow the Park Service recommendations of packing out whatever you pack into the remote country. Old garbage pits teach bears to associate food with people. Bury no food in the wilderness and keep the trailsides clean.

Then the bears will have to return to their natural ways of life, living off the land as bears were intended to do. If you do see such a bear, it is likely to be a respectable wild one, not a half-tame clown that grew up as a beggar.

Chapter 9

WOLVERINES TRAVEL ALONE

The setting sun cast long shadows across the valley before us as the yellow campfire added a comforting warmth to the scene. I sat in front of my tent talking with a long-time Alaskan about one of the wildest of all the creatures in the American outdoors. Bit by bit I had been piecing together the strange story of the animal's life. "Have you, in your lifetime up here," I asked the old hunter, "ever seen many wolverines?"

"Maybe six or seven," he said. "You don't often see them rascals. More often you just see what mischief they've been up to. They're the meanest, orneryest animals ever put on earth."

For some time, the old hunter talked about wolverines. The only trouble was that most of what he said had been said before, and some of the stories about these creatures are not very accurate. Across the North Country the wolverine inspires storytellers.

Only the day before, I had listened to a trapper tell

of the wolverine that put him out of business. "I was setting out my trap line for the winter," he said. "When I came back to run the traps, the first one was set off and there wasn't anything in it. The second was the same way, so was the third, and fourth, and all the rest. I found some tracks and that's how I knew I was in for trouble. A wolverine had followed me along all the time I was setting my traps and plain unset 'em. He put me out of business as far as that place was concerned."

There is no question that they rob traps. Other trappers had also told me that wolverines robbed their traps and stole everything they managed to catch. Almost universally, they are viewed as bad neighbors.

What is it about the wolverine that arouses strong feelings? Competition may be a factor. Some hunters consider wild predators bad because they hunt the same things men hunt. But the wolverine belongs out there in its wild home. It is a wonderful elusive citizen of the wilderness and can take care of itself in a harsh environment.

If you are ever fortunate enough to see a wolverine, you will notice that he has a broad low-slung body—and a low center of gravity. His short legs end in oversized feet. These are his snowshoes, helping him across the white winter landscape. On these short legs he seems to heave himself along, bumping up and down as he goes.

Sometimes he will stand up on his hind feet until some folks say he looks like a little bear. Others may say he looks like a big skunk. But more than anything,

The wolverine has a powerful low-slung body. (Henry Harmon, (U. S. Fish and Wildlife Service)

he looks like a wolverine. He has the short face and little ears found on most mammals of the cold regions.

His shaggy fur coat is dark brownish in color. Along either side he wears a light-colored stripe that reaches from head to tail. But if this is a racing stripe, it's wasted on the wolverine. Even when he thinks he's running fast, he is only loping along at about ten miles an hour.

When grown, the wolverine stands about a foot and a half high at the shoulders, is about forty inches long and weighs perhaps thirty pounds. A member of the weasel clan, he is the largest of all the mustelids, except for the heavier sea otter.

Geese fly in flocks, wolves run in packs, and sea otters live in close touch with others of their kind, but the grumpy wolverine is having none of this togetherness. He is his own creature, a loner, pure and simple. It may be that he is too mean-tempered to live with any other animal, especially another nasty-tempered wolverine. He is a great traveler, out the year around, mostly at night, sometimes making a grand loop of fifty miles.

Only near the end of winter, usually in March, will the males and females get together for the breeding season. The female wolverine will select her denning place in a thicket or rock pile and, in June or July, usually give birth to two or three young.

The young wolverines grow rapidly. They stay with their mother through that summer. Then, in fall the family splits up again. There are no family reunions and no tears at the parting. All through the summer the father of the young has been off on his own business, leaving the family chores to the female.

She would seem to need no help. She leads the young on food-gathering field trips and teaches them two of their most important lessons. One is that almost anything alive, or that may have been alive, is good food for a wolverine. There is one exception, the porcupine. Wolverines will eat their spiny, slow-witted neighbors—but sometimes the porcupine needles kill the wolverine.

Also, the young wolverines must learn to fight. Their mother sets them an example. She doesn't bluff, especially while she is protecting her cubs, she will fight off almost any creature, large or small. There is no record of wolverines attacking humans. But they could hardly be blamed if they did because man is their worst enemy, and most of the time their only enemy.

When a wolverine wants to do something, he wants to do it with all his might. He is perhaps the strongest animal for his size in the north. When he wants to move a rock or drag a chunk of meat across the tundra, he uses every muscle he can bring to the job, pushing, pulling, clawing, shoving, and all the time grunting with the effort. Like an ant, the wolverine seems capable of moving objects several times its weight. One wolverine is known to have dragged a dead Dall sheep a mile and a half across the rough open country of Mount McKinley National Park although he weighed only one fifth as much as the sheep.

One North Country trapper left his cabin in the middle of winter. He had often heard that wolverines are skilled at breaking into untended cabins. Where could he store his groceries to keep them safe while he was away? Outside was a high stack of firewood, so he stored his food on top of the woodpile. Surely the wolverine could not find a way straight up the sides of the woodpile.

When the trapper returned, he found the wolverine had been there, climbed the woodpile, torn open the food box and eaten what he wanted. In the process some crumbs apparently filtered down through the woodpile. Did the wolverine settle for the feast spread out before him? Hardly! Instead, he could think only of those scraps that had fallen down out of reach, so he tore down the woodpile. Sadly, the trapper restacked his winter's wood supply.

A wolverine will even steal from the grizzly bear. A government trapper once told me of setting traps to catch a stock-killing bear in the mountains of Montana. Instead, to his surprise, he caught a wolverine. Everyone thought the wolverines were all gone from those mountains until this one took over the bear's kill.

What would prompt a wolverine to tackle a bear? Perhaps the wolverine does not realize that the bear outweighs him by several hundred pounds. The bear may look up from his meal and rushing right at him, in that clumsy loping run, is the wolverine, an angry ball of fur all filled with teeth and long claws. The grizzly may grab the impudent little invader, bite him through the head, then swat him into left field. At other times he is said to turn and lope away leaving the food to the snarling wolverine.

The wolverines are now almost gone from our western mountains.
(Henry Harmon, U. S. Fish and Wildlife Service)

Wolverines have been known to attack and kill deer and even small moose, most likely when these large animals are bogged down in deep snow and unable to run or fight back. One was observed trying to drag away an entire quarter of a moose.

Northern trappers place a high value on the fur of the wolverine. Once I asked an Eskimo in the Canadian Arctic what kind of fur rimmed the parka hood he wore. "Wolverine," he said. His face lighted up proudly. Dog fur is a common substitute but wolverine is the best of all. It is sometimes said this is because frost will not form on wolverine fur, but this is not true. However, frost can be easily brushed off this remarkable fur, leaving it clean and dry.

Trouble has faced the wolverine since European man first arrived in North America. Tough customers or not, the wolverines cannot win against man. Gradually, they have given ground. They are now almost gone from our western mountains. In the far North as well they will surely vanish unless given rigid protection.

Wolverines have been kept in zoos, but living in cages they seem to lose their fighting spirit. Far from their native wilderness, no longer forced to live by their strength, it is said that they may become rather sweet-natured. It seems almost a shame.

Chapter 10

A DIGGING CHAMPION

One afternoon, when I least expected it, I met a badger face to face. I was driving along an unpaved country road in the Big Hole Valley in western Montana. The badger had come out beside the road and stood on its ridiculously short legs beneath a barbed wire fence watching me as I came to a halt. Until then I had never seen one of these creatures go into its famous digging act. Here was my chance.

I looked for its den and saw a mound of earth more than a hundred yards away. The badger was already heading for home when I crossed the fence. A badger is not built for speed. When it runs, it waddles. As it tried to escape on those short legs it looked like a lump of fur rippling across the prairie. It was doing its best, but even at top speed it was making only five or six miles an hour.

By running around the animal, I managed to place myself in its path, being careful to keep my distance. The badger tried to turn aside and again I cut off its escape route. Then it happened. The badger began digging so fast it seemed to turn itself up on end, and its body began to disappear into the earth.

When a badger digs, it uses every tool at its command. Those front feet carry long, sharp claws and the strong shoulder muscles drive them at high speeds. Meanwhile, it uses its mouth to help loosen the earth. The front feet move earth back beneath the body and the back feet kick it on out of the tunnel. In a few minutes, with a shower of earth flying four or five feet into the air, the badger had vanished into a hole about fourteen inches wide. A creature capable of digging at that speed is safe almost anywhere. It needs only to put its digging tools to work and create an instant tunnel.

This creature with the marvelous digging skills is a large member of the weasel family. A big badger may weigh twenty pounds, be two feet long and look almost as wide. It wears a loose-fitting coat of shaggy fur that is silvery gray in color. Its pointed face is marked with dark lines running up across its head to its shoulders.

Badgers are found from Michigan and Ohio westward, and from Canada south to Mexico. Badgers are rare in Ohio, but some years ago one was found in the basement of an Ohio home. It created a problem because it was not welcome in the basement. But it did not volunteer to come out into the open, and the concrete floor prevented it from digging. The owner first sent his dog in to chase the badger out. Instead, the badger chased the dog out. Next, various men of the neighborhood tried, and each of them came rushing out.

The badger was watching me as I came to a halt. (George Laycock)

Only by killing the animal could thcy they finally remove it from the basement.

Badgers are like that in a fight. Many a dog has learned the hard way not to fight with a badger. Its long, curving claws are fearsome weapons, and it has a steel-trap bite. As it fights, the badger snaps and snarls in a ferocious manner and the dog wants to be somewhere else. Even the badger's coat gives it protection. The fur is so coarse and loose-fitting that other creatures have a hard time getting a hold on the badger.

Badgers eat ground squirrels, gophers, moles, mice, and insects. There are times when the badger may even catch and consume a skunk. Rattlesnakes are lunch meat to a badger, especially when the reptile is found immobile during winter hibernation.

Much of the badger's hunting is done at night. When it must, it digs down to capture other animals in their burrows. As fall approaches, badgers feed more heavily than ever. They build up a thick layer of fat and this helps them through the cold months when food will be scarce. Badgers do not, however, go into true hibernation. Instead, they curl up in a den at the end of their burrow and drift into a deep sleep from which they may awaken during the winter if they become too hungry for comfort. By sleeping through much of the winter they need less food. Sometimes if a badger kills more food than it needs, it buries the surplus for a snack later.

Life for the infant badger begins in early spring. From one to five youngsters are born on a bed of soft dry grass, six or eight feet underground in a burrow that may be thirty-five feet long. There it is dark, quiet,

The badger's pointed head is marked with a white line running up the middle of its face from its nose to the top of its head. (Luther C. Goldman, U. S. Fish and Wildlife Service)

The badger can dig its prey out of burrows. (E. P. Haddon, U. S. Fish and Wildlife Service)

and comfortable. The old male badger is nowhere around. He leaves the rearing of the young to the female.

After the young are about a month old, their mother weans them. Then, instead of feeding them on milk, she brings them delicacies collected on her hunting trips. Now the young ones grow rapidly. When they are about two-thirds the size of their mother, she brings them out into the sunshine where they romp and play and begin to accompany her on hunting trips. By autumn these young badgers are about as large as their parents and capable of taking care of themselves. The female's home duties are over. But in August or September she probably mates again and she will raise a new family the following year.

In spite of their feeding habits, badgers are usually unloved by ranchers and farmers who do not like all those holes dug in their fields. A running horse can step in a badger hole, fall, and send its rider tumbling into the sagebrush. And as he limps off after his horse, the rider says bad things about badgers. Even if this doesn't happen, most ranchers worry because it might. Sometimes a tractor or mowing machine can drop a wheel into a badger hole and suffer damage.

Although they have reputations as fighters, badgers are playful. In captivity, they will play with balls and other toys much as a kitten or puppy might. They may make friends with other animals, even ones that might be their enemies out in the wild.

Chapter 11

SOCIABLE SEA OTTERS

From the shallow water near the seashore, a dark little head decorated with beady black eyes and long whiskers, popped suddenly from the water. For a brief time the animal seemed to stand in the water on some submerged rock while surveying the scene around him. On shore, surprised tourists yelled to each other and pointed. What would this strange creature do next? It did not take them long to find out.

Its eyesight is poor but the sea otter noticed the movement. It dipped from sight so quietly and gracefully that it left scarcely a ripple to mark the spot where it had appeared.

Beneath the surface, the rare creature, using big webbed hind feet, pushed itself forward at full speed. It continued to paddle as fast as it could, came to the surface for air, and once more the people saw it. But this time it was more than one hundred feet farther out to sea. The otter flipped onto its back and paddled steadily away from shore. Finally, when nearly a thousand feet away, it relaxed.

It stood again in the water and looked around. While the people watched with binoculars, it popped from sight and popped up again, twisting, turning, rolling, diving—the supreme aquatic acrobat. The ocean was the world it knew well. Here was safety, food, security. Finally, it rested, floating on its back, rocking easily in the gentle waves.

The sea otter has always worn a coat far too valuable for its own good. As long as men have known about the fur that covers this seagoing member of the weasel family, they have coveted it. These furs have sold for as much as twenty-seven hundred dollars each. The sea otter's fur is unbelievably soft, and so dense that it keeps the cold sea water away from the otter's skin. While many mammals living in the ocean are protected by thick layers of fat, the sea otter's fur holds a blanket of air for insulation. Males are four and a half feet long and sometimes weigh eighty pounds.

Big trouble for the sea otter began in 1741. That year the Russian Czar sent Captain Commander Vitus Bering out to explore the North Pacific. Shipwrecked for the winter on one of the Aleutian Islands, Bering and his crew ate the playful otters, then saved their beautiful furs. The following spring, their boat rebuilt, the explorers returned to their own country. With them went the first sea otter furs to reach the civilized world.

Before long other ships came, big ships and little ships, and all carried crews of hunters determined to

The sea otter has always worn a coat far too valuable for its own good. (George Laycock)

search out the fabled otters and grow rich on their furs.

With clubs, stones, and guns they chased the sea otters, killing every one they could. Females with young were taken. Entire colonies of otters were wiped out.

The Russians, always searching for more furs, moved far down the coast and built Fort Ross, eighty-eight miles north of San Francisco. You can see it there in a state park today. But after twenty-nine years of searching the California coast for furs, they found that the sea otter supplies were dwindling.

By 1900 the once abundant sea otters were nearly gone. None were any longer seen along the California shore. In the Aleutian Islands there were perhaps only five hundred alive. But still there was no law to protect them. Only in 1911, when it was almost too late, did the United States, Japan, and Russia sign a treaty bringing them protection.

With sea otters nearly gone, Russia could see no further need for its vast Alaskan territory. In 1867 Alaska was sold to the United States for $7,200,000, two cents an acre!

Finally, in 1913, the United States turned the Aleutian Islands into a National Wildlife Refuge, and the sea otter was given full protection. Gradually, the otters began to increase again and move back from the edge of extinction. Men learned more about these animals over the years. They began to realize that the sea otter is one of the world's most amazing wild creatures.

The otter lives in the shallow ocean shelf near the shore where it can easily dive to the bottom for its food. It eats such foods as clams, snails, crabs, sea urchins, and small fish. When it comes up from its deep sea pantry carrying a mussel, snail, or sea urchin, it will flip over and float on its back. Sometimes it may also carry a flat rock which it lays on its chest. Then, gripping the shellfish in its paws, the sea otter bangs it down on the rock repeatedly until the shell cracks open. Now it is an easy matter to pick out the juicy prize.

How does a sea otter sleep? It seldom comes ashore. Instead, it sleeps on its back, floating on the surface, and rocking on the dark rippling waters, anchored in place by a strand of seaweed placed across its chest. The mother sea otter may even sleep in this position with her young one clasped to her breast.

A female sea otter produces only one young otter every second year. She is an excellent mother who seldom leaves her baby far from her reach unless she must leave it floating solo on the surface while she dives for food. Sometimes she carries her baby along on these underwater adventures.

For many years the sea otters were believed all gone from California, but in 1938, near Monterey, a man stood on a cliff and looked down on the bay. He saw there a group of strange dark-colored animals bobbing and playing in the kelp bed. The sea otters had returned.

If you travel along that coast today, you may see one or more of these famous animals. One of the best of all places for sea otter watching is Point Lobos State Reserve near Carmel.

Meanwhile, in Alaska, there are now many thousands of them. Sometimes their numbers grow so high the government again permits a few to be taken for their furs. Or they may be caught alive and moved to new homes where sea otters once lived and where men killed them. In this way the amazing and intelligent sea otter has returned to some of its native waters.

Chapter 12

THE ELUSIVE CAT

In a little town in eastern Montana one afternoon, I walked past an automobile, empty except for a pet in the back seat. At first glance the yellowish brown animal appeared to be an overgrown house cat. On second look, I noticed a collar around its neck and a strong chain. I leaned close to the window of the tightly locked car for a look at the attractive cat.

Instantly a flurry of fangs, fully extended claws, flying feet, and cat fur slammed against the window, inches from my face. Glinting eyes, opened jaws, and an angry cascade of growls, snarls, and hisses sent me leaping back.

It happened very rapidly. Bobcats move like fur-covered lightning, and it obviously was not afraid of me in spite of the fact that I towered over it and weighed six or seven times as much as it did. If it had not been for the sheet of plate glass, and perhaps the chain, I would have had a face full of bobcat claws.

So rapidly had the cat attacked that, in my reflex

The automobile was empty except for a pet in the back seat. (George Laycock)

escape effort, I banged against another car. As I rubbed my bruised elbow, a gangling rancher in blue jeans and cowboy boots came from the store. "Don't let it worry you," he said, smiling, "just because you didn't make a hit with 'Sonny Boy.' He never does warm up much to people. We took him from his mama before his eyes were open, or I reckon we couldn't get along with him ourselves." Thoughtfully, the rancher paused. "I guess you couldn't say he really has much love for us either," he added. "Bobcats make interesting pets all right, but I never heard of one taming to where you could trust him completely."

Several people he knew had tried to keep them. Many had taken them to the local veterinarian to have fangs and claws removed. But the bobcat wants to be its own boss and does not surrender its independence or freedom lightly. The only serious enemy it has is man, and if they were to meet on equal terms, a twenty-five-pound bobcat would probably turn a two-hundred-pound man into a promising track star. If you hear it said of a man, "He can lick his weight in bobcats," don't you believe it.

But the bobcat does not go around looking for trouble. Cautious, elusive, secretive—it slips through the thickets like the born hunter it is. If it has its way, you will never catch a glimpse of it. Traveling mostly at night, it is ready, by daylight, to hole up in some tangled thicket or under a rocky ledge and rest.

As evening comes on, it rises from this bed, stretches, yawns, and begins to inspect the landscape. A slight movement may mean food. During the night, it may travel five miles or more. Its hearing is good but not spectacular. Its sense of smell is no match for that of the black bear or the white-tailed deer. The bobcat's biggest aids in finding prey are its hunting skill and its sight. It has excellent night vision.

When hunting, the bobcat will often slip to the top of a rise, and, very slowly and gently lift itself high enough to peek over the ridge and see what awaits it on the other side. If it catches a glimpse of a rabbit, mouse, squirrel, or bird, it may lower itself until its body hugs the ground. Then, taking one silent step at a time, it inches into range. Finally, it bounds from the leaves and grass and, in a single leap or two, is upon its prey. If it misses, it seldom chases the frantic creature far. Instead it begins to search for another.

Bobcats live in many parts of the country. Some live out their lives in the deep swamps of Florida and other southeastern states. Others are desert dwellers. Bobcats are at home in the lower slopes of the mountain ranges too, and especially in those regions where there are broken areas of trees, brush, and rocky outcroppings. They are found from the Atlantic to the Pacific and from Mexico to Canada. Farther north, however, where winters are bitterly cold, bobcats become scarce and gradually the larger Canada lynx takes over.

Biologists believe that there may be more bobcats today than before the country was settled. The clearing of the forests was good for many of the creatures on which the bobcats feed, and consequently for the cats themselves.

The bobcat resembles an oversized house cat. (Woodrow Goodpaster)

If you were to meet a bobcat on the trail, you would notice at once that it looks like an oversized house cat that got his tail caught in a lawnmower. The average bobcat weighs about twenty-five to thirty pounds, and is thirty inches long. The male is generally bigger than the female. Bobcats may look bigger than they are because of their fluffy fur coats. Their legs are long, and their ears are decorated with tufts of fur that biologists believe help them hear better.

Ordinary house cats that people have abandoned sometimes grow so big they are mistaken for bobcats. Some years ago I went with a naturalist friend to examine a cat killed by a neighboring farmer. Both the farmer and the game warden thought it was a bobcat. The cat's skin was nailed to the garage door, and indeed it looked big enough to have been worn by a bobcat. But the color was not right, the tail was too long, and the ear tufts were not as they should be. And, for a clincher, the teeth were those of a house cat and not a bobcat.

During March, when bobcats are in the mating season, they become wandering, restless travelers. And they fill the night with squalling and howling.

For a nursery the female locates a secret hideaway in a rocky den or hollow log. Ordinarily, she will have two or three kittens about sixty-two days after she has mated. They are born blind and helpless, but fully robed in soft fur coats, and for nine days their eyes remain closed.

As they grow older, the wild kittens seem to be enjoying life. Like kittens anywhere, they are active and playful. But remember that even when young, they are equipped with sharp claws and nasty tempers. One Pennsylvania hunter recalls painfully the day he decided to pick up a baby bobcat. He reached among them and just as he did, the enraged kittens scrambled over his hand like a swarm of giant bumblebees. The hand looked as though it had fought a meat grinder—and lost. Young bobcats, like the young of all wildlife, should be left alone.

When they're about two months old, the kittens are weaned, but they still stay with their mother through the remainder of the summer. Mother and young wander together through the warm nights, searching for food and learning to hunt. By their first autumn the young cats have left their mother's company. But the brothers and sisters may spend their first winter together.

If bobcats do not like people, who could blame them? Most people look on bobcats as enemies because the bobcats take some things, especially rabbits and game birds, that men want for themselves. Bobcats have been known to kill full-sized deer. And on rare occasions, they may turn to the sheep lot or the turkey pens.

For years men in some places have put a price on the bobcat's head. Traps are set, and the bounty hunters carry dead bobcats to town to collect the rewards. This seems unfortunate for a couple of reasons. First, the bounty system has been ineffective in controlling bobcats. There may be more of them today than ever. Besides, the bobcat has its vital predator's role to play in the wild community. Anyway you look at the bobcat it is interesting, strong, and self-reliant. It asks no favors and offers none. It is a model of raw courage and fighting spirit, and has been since before men invaded its range.

Perhaps the most unusual case of a human attack on a bobcat was reported some time ago from Missouri where a man surprised a bobcat and scared it into jumping out of a tree. As the cat loped away, the man began imitating the barking of a hound. Instead of running faster, the bobcat wheeled and turned to fight the "dog." The only weapon the startled man was carrying was a claw hammer. He took aim and threw the hammer at the rapidly approaching cat with all his might. It caught the bobcat right between the eyes, dropping him dead on the spot.

That's the way it is for the bobcat—from birth to death, it is one hard knock after the other. But the bobcat is a tough scrapper and never begs for mercy. And you can't help respecting a creature like that.

Chapter 13

THE AMERICAN LION

Some years ago folks around our farm community were absolutely certain there was a cougar or mountain lion running wild in the fields and woods, where no cougar had been known to live for many decades. This is not unusual. An entire community can be terrorized by a cougar that is not there at all.

This story began with a scream in the night. There is a common belief that all cougars scream a lot in the night. Experienced cougar hunters doubt this and claim they almost never hear a cougar scream, night or day. To others, however, the squalling of a bobcat or house cat, somehow becomes the "scream of a cougar."

Unfortunately, today the cougar is gone from large areas of its original range. If you were to catch even a fleeting glimpse of a wild cougar, or even find its tracks, you could consider yourself among the most fortunate outdoorsmen.

There never was a time when cougars were abundant in the sense that rabbits or bobwhites are plentiful.

The cougar is gone from large areas of its original range. (George Laycock, Courtesy of the Denver Museum of Natural History)

The cougar needs a big hunting territory of many square miles through which it roams.

In its original range the cougar occupied more territory than any other mammal in North or South America. Its native land stretched from southeastern Alaska to the Atlantic Coast and southward all the way to the southern tip of South America. It lived in the jungles, deserts, forested hills, and in the mountains at elevations up to several thousand feet above sea level.

One might think that a wild creature this versatile could survive a lot of pressure. But men and cougars have been enemies for a long time, and the cougars have been the losers. No one argues the fact that the cougar, which may measure six feet in length and weigh 175 pounds or more, will stalk and kill large prey when hungry. The deer is to the cougar what mice are to the pet house cat—lunch.

This does not mean, however, that the hunting cougar will not accept substitutes, including a calf or a colt. These eating habits have caused cougars trouble with ranchers and farmers and led men to kill cougars with the aid of guns, dogs, traps, and poisons. As a result these magnificent big American cats have dwindled and vanished from region after region.

Some biologists now believe that once these remarkable big cats were more numerous in the eastern forests than in the western mountains. The eastern forests were cut over as the country was settled, and as the forests vanished so did the white-tailed deer. Deer were a major food for the cougar, and like the deer and the forests, it, too, was in trouble. The trees have come back. So have the deer. But the elusive, wilderness-loving cougar has not.

If you were to see a cougar, the chances are good that you would recognize this big cat at once. It wears a plain, yellowish tan coat of short fur, somewhat darker above than on its belly. It is a slender creature with a deep body, a small head, and long tail.

Cougar kittens are usually born between April and August, from ninety-one to ninety-seven days after the mating. The newly born kittens, averaging two to the litter, weigh perhaps a pound each and are about a foot long. Their eyes are closed during the first days of their lives. Their first coats are spotted with black markings. By the time they are a year old they should weigh around fifty pounds but may still be traveling with their mother. From her the kittens learn the fine points of hunting for a living. The cougar is not particular about its choice of prey. It takes what is available.

Like its smaller cousins, the house cat and bobcat, the cougar stalks its prey until it is within striking range. Then, in a sudden bounding rush, it takes the animal by complete surprise. If it kills a large animal, the cougar may drag what it cannot eat into hiding and return later for a second helping.

There is not much point in people worrying about being attacked by a cougar. Cases of cougar attacks on humans are extremely rare. These big cats apparently consider humans unfit to eat.

If allowed to live out its natural life, the cougar may roam its territory for a dozen years or more. One

The cougar stalks its prey silently until it is within striking range.
(U. S. Fish and Wildlife Service)

held in captivity is known to have survived eighteen years.

For many years no laws protected the cougar. But in recent times some states have extended protection to this native American by adding it to the official roster of game animals. They are then no longer "varmints" to be shot on sight. Wildlife officials can protect them by closed seasons. This magnificent wild hunter deserves our protection.

Chapter 14

SEALS AND THEIR FUR COATS

In the water the seals move with a beauty and grace that few wild creatures anywhere can equal. These are the finfeet. Turning, twisting, and diving, they cut through the water at high speed, driven by the strangely shaped feet which have become broad leathery paddles. So at home are they in the water that even when diving they hardly make a splash.

But seals come out of the water too, and when they do they give up their graceful movements. Now they can only waddle and drag their heavy bodies over rocks or sand. The sea is always the safety zone where they feel secure. If enemies approach, they drag themselves back down toward the sea as rapidly as they can.

Spread around the world are thirty-two species of seals, all of them large creatures, at home in the oceans. One family of them, known as the eared seals, contains the fur seal and the sea lion. All the rest belong to the larger family of true seals.

Seals come out of the water to have their young. (V. B. Scheffer, U. S. Fish and Wildlife Service)

Protecting these animals from the cold ocean waters is a thick coat of remarkable hair, a fur so valuable that for centuries men have taken it from them and turned it to their own use. This taking of seals for fur causes arguments between people who want the furs for ladies' coats and others who insist that the killing of all seals should stop. The proper answer may depend on the kind of seals involved, whether it is the fur seal of Alaska or the harp seal of the North Atlantic.

The adult harp seals are dark gray in color, and the males weigh between six hundred and eight hundred pounds. But the petite females weigh perhaps one hundred pounds. The harp seal spends its summers cruising and fishing off the shores of Greenland.

These seals move south in autumn. One group of them spends the winters along the rugged rocky coast of Newfoundland. Another group moves on southward into the Gulf of St. Lawrence and there, for more than a century and a half, sealers have met them to make their kill late in February.

During those bitter weeks of midwinter, the females haul themselves out of the water and up onto the ice floes to give birth to their pups. They have only one pup each. The pup is a fluffy white ball of fur with black button eyes. It is their white fur that the industry demands, and lying on the ice these infants are helpless.

For two weeks the pups have gorged on milk that is half butterfat and have increased in weight from twenty-five pounds to perhaps one hundred pounds. After that their white coats are quickly replaced by

The sea lion is related to the fur seal. (George Laycock)

darker colors. So the sealers move fast and, while the white pups lie helpless in their icy nurseries, the men kill them with clubs. Then they skin them, and haul their furs off in bundles to waiting ships.

In 1964 Canada set limits on the number of young harp seals that could be killed in the Gulf of St. Lawrence. Canadian biologists believe the annual production of young has fallen, and that the seal populations are being drained too rapidly. The quotas for 1971 were 245,000 for Canada and Norway, but some biologists felt that this figure should be cut in half. Around the world people have asked Canada to save the white seal pups.

But in Alaska the story of the fur seals is different. The fur seal's troubles with man began in 1786 when Russia discovered the Pribilof Islands off the Alaskan mainland. Perhaps four million fur seals spent their summers on those islands. For winter the females and young would migrate southward all the way to California, just as they do today.

Then in spring they would begin moving restlessly back toward the Pribilofs. First, from the nearby Gulf of Alaska, came the old males, ponderous, ill-tempered creatures weighing about six hundred pounds. The strongest of them establish breeding territories along the beaches in the Pribilofs. The rest of the summer they stand constant guard and fight with other males to protect their territories.

In June the females arrive, and the males herd as many as possible into their harems. They may average forty mates each. The male guarding his territory goes without food all summer long.

Farther back beyond the beaches the males that do not have territories to defend, form bachelor clubs. These are the seals killed for fur. But before we cry out to stop this fur harvest we should look at the difference between the situation with the harp seals of eastern Canada and these fur seals of Alaska.

When the United States purchased Alaska, millions of seals had already been killed. In the next forty years another two million were killed under government permits. Meanwhile, on the open seas, sealers from the United States, Canada, Japan, and Russia, shot and harpooned the fur seal, killing males, females, and young.

In this way the fur seal quickly approached extinction. By 1911, where once millions of seals came to the Pribilofs, there were perhaps 130,000 remaining. That year the United States, Great Britain, Japan, and Russia signed an international agreement to save the seals.

Killing of the fur seals in the open ocean stopped. Those taken on the Pribilofs were mostly the nonbreeding males, and the numbers killed were closely controlled. The fur seals began to rebuild their numbers. Today the herd once more numbers one and a half million and the fur seals of the Pribilofs are no longer rare.

If all killing of the surplus fur seals on the Pribilofs were stopped, the international agreement would be broken. Then killing would probably start again on the

An Alaskan seal pup. (John Vania, Alaska Department of Fish and Game)

open seas. The fur seal would once more be in grave danger. Instead of being a vigorous thriving herd, scientifically managed, it would almost certainly move once more toward extinction.

Leading conservation organizations say we should not change the scientific plan by which we manage Alaska's fur seals.

Fur seals and harp seals are not the same. And saving one will not help the other. No matter how much we might demand that the fur seals no longer be killed in Alaska, this would not help the white baby harp seals that live in the Atlantic. Each needs its own plan of management.

Chapter 15

THE WHITE-TAILED DEER

Here and there in the mammal world one encounters a happy story. Consider the case of the graceful white-tailed deer which have returned to states where they were once thought to be gone forever. So abundant have deer become that in some neighborhoods they are pests. They eat fruit trees, chase pets, bang into automobiles, and blunder into houses.

In Duluth, Minnesota, for example, they tell of the young white-tailed buck that took a ride in the paddy wagon. This animal wandered down from the hills into a residential section and, instead of eating a few flowers and going back home, he made a wrong turn and headed downtown.

Crowds of children and dogs were soon chasing him. Police cars joined in. Eventually the deer was exhausted and fell on the street.

Police quickly surrounded him, pounced on him, and held him down. They tied him with ropes. Then they lifted him into the police wagon and headed for the

The graceful white-tailed deer have become abundant in some places. (Michigan Department of Conservation)

zoo. Once the buck adapted to zoo life, things went well for him. All year he had plenty to eat, and never again did he have to go downtown into the shopping district.

Life for the white-tailed deer generally begins in early summer when the soft warmth of June brings lush growth to fields and forests. The female, known as the doe, often has twin fawns, and she hides them in brushy places where they may lie perfectly still even when a man or dog comes very close. Their brown coats spotted with white are camouflaged in the sun-dappled forest. A fawn alone in the brush is not lost. Several times a day the mother returns to nurse it. Then, as the youngster reaches an age of four or five weeks, it begins to follow the doe on her nighttime feeding trips.

Leaves, twigs, acorns, fruit, and mushrooms are food for the deer. When full grown, the buck may weigh as much as three hundred pounds in the northern states. Farther south the white-tailed deer are smaller. The smallest of all are the little deer of the Florida Keys, tiny creatures scarcely bigger than a collie dog and weighing perhaps sixty pounds. But wherever they live, the white-tailed deer are nimble, graceful creatures.

One Pennsylvania game protector reported a deer that came into town and visited a ladies' dress shop. The deer dashed down an alley, bolted across Main Street, and with a magnificent leap, soared through a plate glass window and landed inside a clothing factory amid the broken glass.

The deer leaped to its feet and dashed the length of the workroom between two rows of sewing machines.

The fawn's brown coat, spotted with white, is camouflaged in the forest. (Michigan Department of Conservation)

Then it leaped through a window at the back of the shop and fell twenty feet to a blacktop driveway. A clean-up man, the only person in the factory at the moment, ran in disbelief toward the window where the deer had disappeared. The man stood speechless as the animal scrambled up, shook its head, and bounded up and over the hill again toward its home.

In Freeport, Maine, the president of a bank returned solemnly from a deer-hunting trip on which he bagged no deer. During his first hour back on the job, a giant white-tailed buck crashed through a big window, raced the length of the bookkeeping department, and ran down into the basement. He had to be roped and carried out.

Many deer have grown accustomed to farm life. A Missouri farmer reported that deer had been swiping corn from his barnyard corn crib. Then one evening the deer looked through the living room window and saw the television. After that, the deer would feed on corn, then watch the evening show on TV, or so the story goes.

Another deer jumped a six-foot-high fence and splashed into a family swimming pool. Game protectors spent two hours lassoing the swimming deer and escorting the dripping animal to the exit.

If there is one part of the modern world where the wild deer repeatedly get into serious trouble, it is along the highways. Where the number of deer killed on the highways shoots upward in winter, one reason may be the salt spread on the roads to prevent icing. One community in Iowa tried placing salt blocks in nearby fields for the deer, to keep salt-hungry animals from getting themselves killed on the highways. In Pennsylvania alone twenty-three hundred deer were killed on highways in the first eleven months of 1973.

Unfortunate motorists who have hit deer know that a full-grown deer can wreck an automobile. A collision with a deer usually costs the motorist at least four or five hundred dollars in repair bills.

Perhaps the most unbelievable deer-versus-car story comes out of Missouri. Near the Busch Wildlife Area a pick-up truck ran full tilt into a trio of deer crossing the road. One of the deer was killed.

The occupants of a following car stopped to look at the dead deer. Hardly had they stepped out onto the highway when a buck came charging from the woods under full steam and rammed their car head on. As if this were not enough, he backed off, gained momentum, and smacked it again. Then he turned and went off into the woods, apparently satisfied that he had helped to even the score.

Some deer can't understand that painted line that runs down the center of the highway. They somehow think of it as an obstacle to be cleared. A Pennsylvania forester watched a deer come to the center line and leap high to clear it. Then two more deer came from the woods and followed the example. Nobody knows quite why a deer would jump over a white line, unless perhaps it is to get on the other side.

The modern hunter is likely to be less familiar with his quarry and his gun than were his pioneering forebearers who depended on wild game for food. Today

A white-tailed buck. (George Laycock)

the taking of a deer becomes a matter of pride. The hunter wants a picture for his family album. One hunter shot a beautiful ten-point buck, the biggest deer he had ever shot. He laid his 30-30 rifle across the massive antlers of his trophy. Then he stepped back to make a picture to show his grandchildren. He adjusted his camera carefully. But as he did so the dazed buck recovered and bounded to his feet. The last the hunter-photographer saw of the buck, the big deer was dashing off through the woods carrying a rifle on his antlers. The hunter never did recover his gun. In fact, he never even got a snapshot.

Deer, however, seem always to be welcome members of the community. They are sleek and beautiful creatures, even if they do cause trouble now and then.

Chapter 16

WILD DEER OF THE FAR NORTH

Years ago, on my first trip into northern Canada, I saw a massive creature with towering antlers appear one afternoon on the ridge above me. For a moment he stood like a statue etched against the blue sky. Then, in long smooth strides the old monarch moved down the slope, not away from me, but directly toward where I waited.

Finally, he trotted past within twenty-five feet of me and never glanced in my direction. He was the wild free spirit of the Arctic as he moved off across the tundra. This was the closest I have been to a wild Barren Ground caribou. On a later trip to the wilderness of northern Alaska I was searching for caribou on their calving grounds.

The caribou is the most abundant big-game animal of the Arctic. But both in Alaska and Canada their numbers have slipped drastically in recent decades. In Alaska, old-timers tell of paddle-wheel steamers on the

The bison has vanished from most of its original range. (Karl H. Maslowski)

Canadian wolf pups are threatened by man's advance. (George Laycock)

Yukon River stopping for hours to allow migrating caribou to swim the river.

In Canada there might have been as many as two million Barren Ground caribou in 1900. But by 1954, by the best caribou count the game managers could get, there were only 670,000. Four years later this number had dropped to an alarming low of 200,000.

Other wildlife species threatened by man's advance have been less fortunate. The passenger pigeon, heath hen, bison, grizzly bear, wolf, and others vanished from much or all of their original range before modern wildlife science could come to their rescue. Today, both in Canada and Alaska, career outdoorsmen are probing the mysteries of the wandering caribou. From such studies are coming ideas for halting the caribou losses and building up their numbers again. Today there are believed to be six hundred thousand Barren Ground caribou in Alaska, and five hundred thousand or more in Canada.

In Fairbanks I talked with the manager of the Arctic National Wildlife Range. He spread out a map of northeastern Alaska. Then, pointing to locations on the map, he told me about the restless caribou that travel back and forth every year crossing the mountains between Alaska and Canada.

In summer they are found in the Arctic National Wildlife Range. By winter they are back in Canada at the edge of the forests. There are an estimated 140,000 caribou in this herd, the second largest herd in all of Alaska. Each spring, in his single engine airplane, the refuge manager crosses the wilderness and searches out the caribou. He estimates their numbers and compares the populations with other years.

But counting caribou is not easy. These animals are on the move throughout their lives. Where they appear one year, they may not show up the following year. He had explained to me that thousands of caribou cows should be on the calving grounds in the foothills of the Brooks Range. Surely, I figured, as I flew northward in a small plane, there would be no problem finding thousands of caribou from the air.

In a little valley pinched between towering gray slopes, I spotted our first caribou, a little group of half a dozen animals. There were no new calves among them. After this, I thought, we should see caribou by the thousands. But throughout the day we saw only a few more animals.

Then the next morning, after camping out in the tundra, we flew across the snow-capped crest of the mountains. We had crossed over to the North Slope which stretches northward down to the Arctic Ocean. There in the foothills we found the caribou.

At first there were a few small groups of three or four animals, some accompanied by new wobbly-legged calves. Eventually, we could see caribou everywhere we looked. They were scattered across thirty miles or more of tundra. Here on the slopes, several miles inland from the icy Arctic Ocean, the ancient herds were being renewed.

In the Arctic the north winds and the biting cold sweep across the snowy fields. But the caribou is equipped for survival in such a world. Its fur coat is

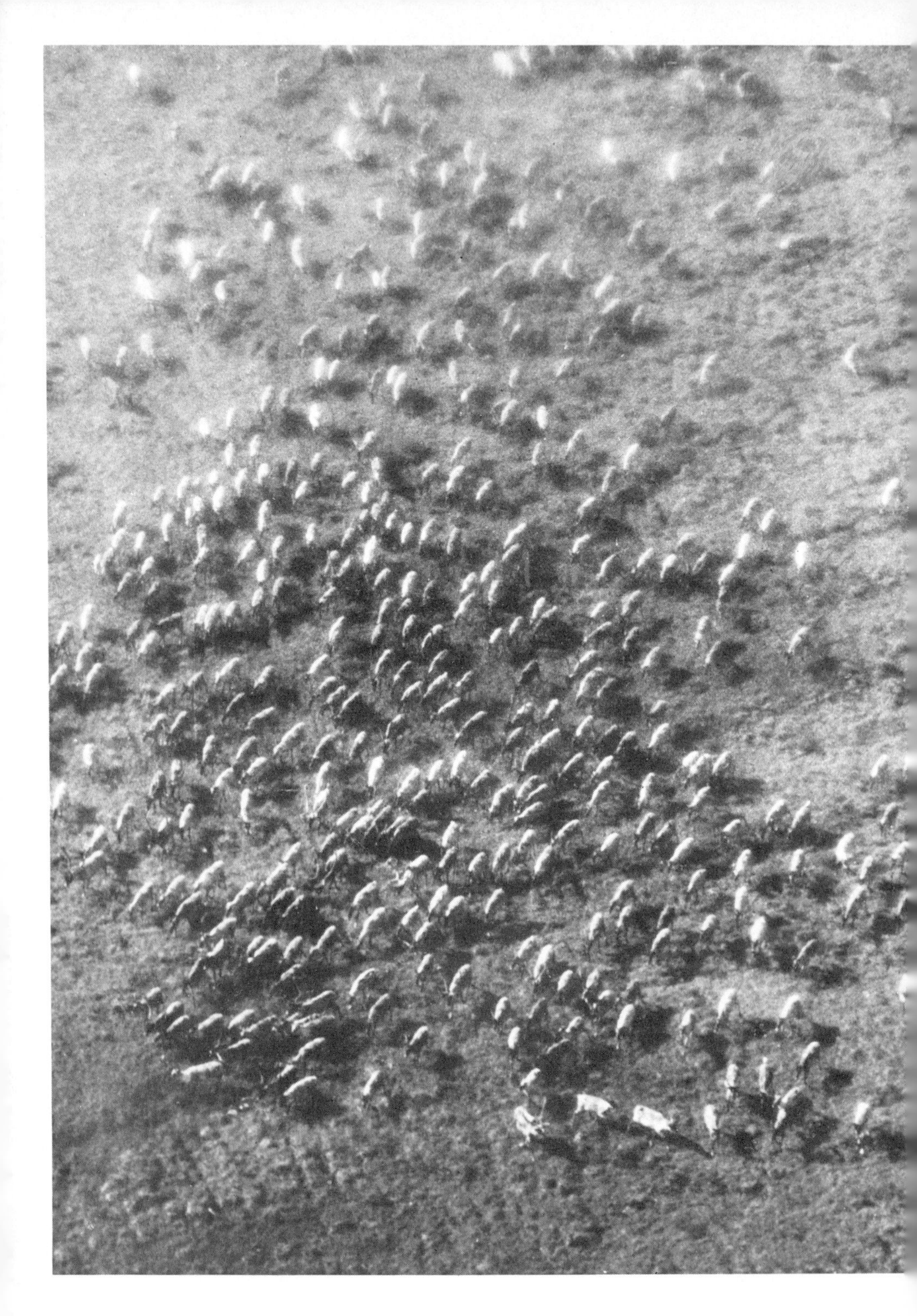

We could see caribou everywhere we looked. (George Laycock)

among the finest in the world. Closely spaced hairs, hollow and filled with insulating dead air, lock out the winter wind. Temperatures may plunge to 50 degrees below zero or lower, and still the caribou is warm and snug in its fur wrap.

The feet of the caribou are broad and spreading. When caribou swim, their broad hoofs become paddles. Meanwhile, the hair, rich in trapped air, is a bouyant life preserver helping to support the animals in the water.

One of the earliest lessons the hunting Eskimo learns is to keep downwind from the caribou. Like deer everywhere, the caribou have a sharp sense of smell. For them, messages of danger ride the winds.

For thousands of years Eskimos and northern Indians lived among the caribou and drew on the great herds for their needs. The caribou herds were their supermarkets. Caribou meat is excellent, but these wild deer of the Arctic provided more than food for the Stone Age man. The bone was fashioned into needles for sewing and also into hide scrapers. Bone was used as well for weapons and to make the bottoms of sled runners hard and smooth. For thread the Eskimo women used the tough sinews taken from the neck and spine of these deer. And teeth pulled from the jaws of the dead caribou became ornaments for the people.

Meanwhile, the fur that protected the wild caribou against the frigid winter winds became clothing to protect the hunter's family too. Seven skins would make a man's suit and, if he was careful, the suit might last for three years. Wearing two suits of caribou hide, one with the warm fur facing inward against his body, the other with the fur outside against the wind, the hunter could stay comfortable in the coldest weather. In addition, the skins were made into kayaks and tents. So many things the people needed came from them that without the caribou, the inland people would have perished.

Before the coming of European man, the Eskimo hunter had only primitive weapons, bone-tipped spears, and bows and arrows. With these he could kill the deer, but only at short range. The best times of the year came for these people during the big migrations when wandering caribou moved over the hills in broad bands that sometimes stretched out for miles.

As the deer advanced, they would pass the hiding places of the women and children who had come out from the little village. And at the right moment the women and children would jump up around the caribou, shouting and waving their arms, and drive them onward toward the waiting hunters, crouched among the rocks.

Another way in which the caribou were hunted was to wait for them where they swam the rivers. With their spears, the men could kill dozens of the animals in a short time. Even these methods failed to reduce the wild deer below what the new calf crops could replace year after year. The caribou survived and so did the people. But then the early traders arrived.

These adventuresome men brought new equipment to the wilderness. There was the rifle, with a reach far greater than that of the spear and the arrow. The number of caribou a man could kill leaped upward.

There was also metal for replacing the bone runner plates on the bottom of the sleds. There were matches and kerosene for tiny stoves. Now a hunter, trapping furs the trader would buy, could travel farther and stay out on the barrens longer than ever before. And because he could kill more deer, he needed a bigger sled and more dogs to pull it. These dogs had to be fed, and this cut still deeper into the caribou numbers.

But even more threatening perhaps was what was happening on the wintering grounds of the caribou. Barren Ground caribou travel southward in autumn toward the northern edge of the forests. Here, among the thin stands of trees, their chief winter food is lichens, sometimes called "reindeer moss."

With their heads lowered, they sniff as they move along until the odor of lichens reaches their sensitive nostrils. Then the caribou bring their snow shovel hoofs into play and quickly paw a hole to reach the food. They feed as they move, gathering a mouthful of food wherever they find it. And where the lichens are abundant, they may quickly harvest the several pounds needed to satisfy their hunger. But where the lichens are not in good supply, they must dig hundreds of holes, work longer for their food, and use more energy to find it.

The lichens on which they survive may stand only a few inches high. But these lichens do not grow to maturity in less than a quarter of a century and sometimes much longer. Wanderlust draws the caribou from region to region, and where they harvest the lichens they may not disturb them again for many years.

But fire, even more than caribou, destroys the lichen growth. After the European man's arrival in the North, fires became increasingly common. In recent times airplanes and boats with outboard motors carried men deeper into the wilderness. I recall seeing a place where a fishing party had enjoyed a shore lunch on the shores of Great Bear Lake. The guide had failed to put the fire out completely. The next day the woods, trees, lichens and all, were still burning. The same thing has happened over thousands of acres across the wintering grounds of the caribou. And where the lichens are burned off, there may be no winter food for the caribou for several decades. Besides, biologists have learned that, strangely, caribou will not cross a recently burned area even to get at good supplies of lichens on the other side.

As for the Arctic National Wildlife Range in northeastern Alaska, this magnificent land is still a wilderness. We found no roads, power lines, or oil wells. These mountains and valleys belong to the wild creatures, including the herds of caribou that come back each year from across the mountains in Canada.

Conservationists hope now that this area, the largest of all our national wildlife refuges, will remain wilderness so the caribou and other wildlife, far up in that northeast corner of Alaska, will always have living space in the cold world that is their home.

Chapter 17

THE OX OF THE ARCTIC

To see a wild musk ox in his native heath you must travel to the Arctic Circle and beyond. Even then you would have trouble locating one because they are so thinly scattered across the vast treeless tundra. Herds of ten or twelve animals are common today only in areas where the musk ox is doing well.

Old records left by early explorers tell us that the herds were once much larger. Samuel Hearne reported in 1795 that as he traveled overland to the Coppermine River he saw musk oxen in herds of eighty to one hundred. Once they were circumpolar. But they have been killed until they are now gone from large areas of their original range. They were extinct in Alaska by the mid-1800s. Today, there are no longer any musk oxen living wild in Alaska except on the Nunivak Island National Wildlife Refuge and a few recent transplants to the mainland. All of these descended from a shipment of thirty-one brought in from Greenland in 1936. In Canada there are an estimated fifteen hundred musk

A wild musk ox on Nunivak Island, Alaska. (Erwin A. Bauer)

oxen running wild on the mainland, with perhaps eighty-five hundred more roaming the cold Arctic islands.

The first to describe the musk ox was a young man named Henry Kelsey, who in 1689 was in the service of the youthful Hudson's Bay Company. Almost from the first, those who saw this Arctic mammal claimed that it gave off a strong odor of musk, especially during the rut when the bulls are competing for females. In later years, in the face of more careful examination and a sharpened olfactory sense, the musk proved to be a myth. But by that time the musk ox, which has no musk glands, had its name, and it still does. Besides, it is not an ox, or even closely related to cattle. The Eskimos simply call him "Oomingmak," the bearded one.

Misnamed or not, the musk ox has gained new fame in recent times. Pioneering stocks of them have been moved from the wilds of their native Arctic ranges and installed in fenced paddocks. One day I drove from Fairbanks, Alaska, out to the University Farm where the University of Alaska and the Institute of Northern Agricultural Research maintained a herd of domestic musk oxen. Behind a six-foot chain-link fence, the contented musk oxen grazed blissfully in tall brome grass pasture. They resembled Shetland ponies, draped in oversized buffalo robes.

Soon I realized what gave these captive animals their strange un-musk ox appearance; they had no horns. I had seen musk oxen in the wild, wearing massive horns that curved down, then up in short graceful lines. This first meeting with a manicured musk ox can be saddening. The wonderful wild look is gone.

The plan to capture and domesticate musk oxen materialized some years ago in the mind of John J. Teal, Jr., a tall, lean Vermonter. In 1954 and 1955, Teal journeyed to the Thelon Game Sanctuary in Canada's Northwest Territories. In his pocket he carried a permit to capture musk ox calves. Earlier efforts to capture them for zoos had proceeded on a simple but brutal plan. The cows were shot and the confused and defenseless calves run down. As the animals became increasingly scarce, however, zoo managers agreed that they would no longer buy calves obtained in this way. The capture of musk ox calves fell off drastically.

Teal captured seven calves by running them into the water, and did this without harming the adult stock. He moved these young musk oxen to his farm in Vermont. He was convinced that this creature could provide a new profitable enterprise for the Eskimos, because the high-grade wool, or qiviut, is considered better than cashmere.

After working with musk oxen about a decade in Vermont, Teal helped establish the herd on the University of Alaska Farm near Fairbanks.

Once the university herd is up to one hundred musk oxen, breeding stock will be lent to Eskimos who want to establish their own domestic herds. Eventually they are to repay with a like number of young animals to start other herds.

Surprisingly, the musk oxen, once brought into captivity, turned out to be extremely easy to tame. Before

Musk ox calves followed the herdsman around hoping to get their noses into a feed bucket. (George Laycock)

the calves are in captivity long, they follow the herdsman around hoping to get their noses into a feed bucket. They come up to the fence to nuzzle visitors. Except for the mature bulls, the herdsman almost never need worry about being attacked.

These captive musk oxen even play their own version of soccer. They butt a huge medicine ball around in the pasture with their heads. It is believed, however, that they still do not choose up sides.

In winter the tame musk oxen are said to enjoy sled riding. When the herdsman pulls a child's sled into one of the fields, the calves sometimes run toward him, jostling for position, each eager for the first ride.

The musk ox is well adapted by nature to its frigid northern climate. Its world is an ice box much of the year, but it moves about in apparent comfort even when temperatures drop to 50 or 60 degrees below zero. Arctic winds rushing across the polar ice cap and down over the tundra buffet its shaggy sides.

I once had the opportunity to examine at close range the hide of a musk ox. It had become a rug. The guard hairs were ten to twelve inches long. Beneath the long outer hairs was a shorter layer of fur so dense it was difficult to separate. The hair of a musk ox is dark brownish black in color, although there is often color variation in geographic races of them, or among individuals because of differences in age.

So completely is the animal covered with this protective hair that only the horns, hoofs, lips, and a spot on the end of the nose are left open to the weather. Naturalists believe that the density of the hair is also the creature's best protection against the hordes of mosquitoes that plague warm-blooded animals across Arctic regions. In summer, musk oxen sometimes gain added protection against insects by facing into the wind or feeding with their faces partially buried among the dwarf willows.

Each year, late in April or in early May, the musk ox begins to lose its fur. Great swatches of it loosen and fall from its shaggy sides to blow across the tundra, hang on the dwarf vegetation and be gathered for nest building material by Arctic birds. The shedding musk ox always gets a new upholstery job by September when the Arctic winter sets in again.

Males and females are similar in appearance. Their dark-colored fur is set off by dirty white socks. Both carry humps on their shoulders and massive sets of horns that cover their skulls and curve down and forward. The broad base of the musk ox horn made it useful as a dipper in the kitchen equipment of the Eskimo woman. To the musk ox the horn is more useful, however, in warding off wolves. Musk oxen apparently enjoy excellent vision. Their hearing likewise is good in spite of the fact that their ears seem small and all but hidden in their fur.

The feet of this Arctic mammal seem especially well adapted to its requirements. On each foot the two hoofs are rather widely separated so that the footprint is wider than it is long. The outer edge of each hoof forms a sharp edge that cuts into hard snow. This is useful when the musk ox must move rapidly to escape natural enemies. But the back part of the hoofs is

A desert bighorn sheep. (George Laycock)

formed into a broad pad, and this provides added traction when the animal must travel steep rocky surfaces. In such situations his amazing agility resembles that of the bighorn sheep. This is not especially surprising to scientists who have decided that musk oxen are relatives of sheep and goats.

The breeding season for the musk ox begins in summer. Then there are resounding battles between the bulls. Like the bighorn sheep the male musk ox stands facing his opponent, then rushes at full force to meet the challenger head on. Horns collide with a smashing impact. Then the two animals turn and square off again, sometimes repeatedly until they tire of the game or one proves weaker and is banished from the herd.

In the wild, a cow usually has one calf every second year. The young musk ox may nurse for as long as fifteen months, which is probably an aid to survival through that first dark winter when food is scarce and difficult for a young animal to find. He will still, however, have become acquainted with the foods of his parents at a tender age, sometimes beginning to pick at the willows and grasses of the Arctic when only four days old.

The front end of a musk ox is much better protected than the rear. At the first appearance of a wolf pack, the little band of musk oxen organize themselves into a circle, facing outward toward the enemy. The attacking wolves meet a circle of horns. In the center of the circle are the calves, sometimes huddling beneath their mothers and entirely hidden by the parents' long flowing hair. An adult musk ox may dash a short distance out of the circle to chase a wolf. But then it backs deliberately into its position again.

One afternoon, while flying across the central Arctic not far from the Arctic Ocean, we spotted a lone musk ox. We circled him at low altitude for a better look and possibly pictures. He dashed off up a steep slope. At the base of a sheer cliff he wheeled and stood his ground challenging our plane and he was still there when we departed.

Primitive people apparently cut heavily into the musk oxen populations. But those who really brought the animal close to oblivion were explorers and hunting parties sent out from whaling crews to find fresh meat.

Aside from the wolf, only the Barren Ground grizzly bear could have been listed among the important threats to the musk ox. They are remarkably free of parasites. Occasionally a musk ox perishes when it falls over a cliff.

Those striving to domesticate it think the destiny of the musk ox is to come in out of the northern wilds and share its valued underwool with people. The idea may work or it may not. But the musk oxen I will remember best are not the creatures robbed of their horns, playing soccer, and going sled riding inside a fence.

Instead, I choose to remember the wild ones, the strong and resourceful musk oxen that for uncounted ages have survived the world's harshest climate.

Chapter 18

WHERE ARE THE MAMMALS HEADED?

If you were to sit very quietly in a prairie dog town in South Dakota late in the evening, and if you were lucky, you might be one of the few living people ever to catch a glimpse of the black-footed ferret. This mammal is a member of the weasel family. It is also one of the world's rarest animals, dangerously close to extinction.

Its legs are short and its body is long and slender like a fur-covered sausage. It has a small, round head with sparkling, little dark eyes covered by a black mask.

What has brought the black-footed ferret so near the end of his days on earth? For one thing, he can't live unless he has other mammals, the prairie dogs, for neighbors. The ferret makes his home in the prairie dog burrows. And when he gets hungry he eats a prairie dog. Life was like this for the ferrets and prairie dogs for hundreds of thousands of years. Only in recent times has their way of life been threatened.

Prairie dogs live in burrows that help protect them from predators. (George Laycock)

Another famous mammal was important in this grassland drama. The great shaggy bison or buffalo grazed across the plains and helped keep the grass short. Short grass was good for the prairie dog, and the prairie dog was good for the black-footed ferret.

Then, along came still another mammal, man, who was not especially good for any of them. He swept across the grasslands through the heart of the continent. First he killed the buffalo by the millions—almost all of them.

Next, men began poisoning the prairie dogs. They claimed that prairie dogs ate grass which sheep should have. They also said the prairie dog burrows might break a horse's leg. All this was bad news for the fat, little prairie dogs sitting outside their burrows barking warnings to their neighbors. It was also bad news for the ferrets.

As for the ferret, unless he gets a lucky break soon, he is certain to become extinct. His name will be written along with the passenger pigeon and other extinct creatures. Around the world 36 species of mammals have become extinct since 1600. Today another 120 species and subspecies are threatened with extinction.

North America has watched many of its wild creatures come to the danger point in the last 200 years. Among them, the monstrous grizzly bears disappeared from state after state. Perhaps only 850 remain today south of the Canadian border. In the Arctic the great white polar bear may also be in trouble. So is the eastern timber wolf, cougar, and the little San Joaquin kit fox in California. And there are others that need

The dark, shaggy bison grazed across the plains. (George Laycock)

The great white polar bear has no enemy but man. (George Lay-cock)

our help if they are to survive. They start down the road to extinction by disappearing from one area after the other. Mammals that adjusted and evolved to meet the new conditions created by slowly changing climates may not change rapidly enough to meet the more swiftly changing modern conditions.

How have we made life impossible for so many of the wild animals? First of all, we have changed their habitat. Where the woodland animals depended on the trees for food and shelter, we cut down the forests. Where the grassland wildlife lived, we burned and plowed the prairies, drained and farmed the marshes and potholes. We have dammed the streams to flood the fertile valleys, and run chemicals, soil, and sewage into the rivers and oceans.

In addition, we brought in foreign animals, such as cattle, horses, sheep, and many more, to turn loose and compete with the wild ones already here.

Meanwhile, we were attacking many kinds of wildlife directly. When the country was first settled there were almost no laws to protect wild animals. Bison were slaughtered, sometimes just for their tongues. Birds were killed to get their feathers for decorating ladies' hats. Eskimo curlews, flying down across the continent in migration, were shot and hauled off to the food market by the wagonload. Prairie chickens, extinct now through most of their original range, were hauled off by the barrel. And so were passenger pigeons. Coyotes, bobcats, prairie dogs, bears, and wolves have all been considered by man to be his enemies, and they have been killed.

But there are some mammals that have lived through all the pressures we have brought to bear on them. Coyotes, although we have poisoned, shot, and trapped them, have spread out into more of the country than ever. The graceful white-tailed deer is perhaps here in greater numbers than when the land was first settled.

As the world around them changes, so do the mammals. We have already changed the world too much for the wolves, grizzly bears, and cougars to continue living in most of the places they once knew.

Could we change it so much that man also could no longer survive? All mammals, man included, like all other living organisms, are part of their ecosystems. When we lose an animal, we should see the warning. The extinction of a wild creature tells us something. In the stories of the mammals, and how they fit the environments on which they depend, is the reminder that man, too, is a living creature. Like other mammals and living creatures everywhere, he depends on a healthy environment.

INDEX

George Laycock has written more than twenty books on natural history and conservation. He has also written several hundred articles for many national magazines, including *Field and Stream, Sports Illustrated, Audubon, National Wildlife, Better Homes and Gardens,* and *Boys' Life*. When he writes of animals and the outdoors, he deals with subjects of lifelong interest. He is a native of Ohio, and holds a degree in wildlife management from The Ohio State University. He has traveled and camped widely, gathering information and taking pictures for his articles and books.